Give Your Gifts!!

Your Sacred Wealth Code

UNLOCK YOUR SOUL BLUEPRINT FOR PURPOSE & PROSPERITY

Love Prema

PREMA LEE GURRERI

Published by Heart Drop Press
P.O. Box 66404, Burien, WA 98166

ISBN-13: 978-0-9987712-0-5

Library of Congress Control Number: 2017903133

www.SacredWealthCode.com
(206) 801-0863

Cover and Layout Design: Bryna René Haynes, www.TheHeartofWriting.com
Editor: Bryna René Haynes, www.TheHeartofWriting.com
Cover photo: Nikki Incandela

Printed in the United States.

Dedication

To every soul who is committed to stepping onto the path of greatness:

May this work open the way to your biggest dreams.

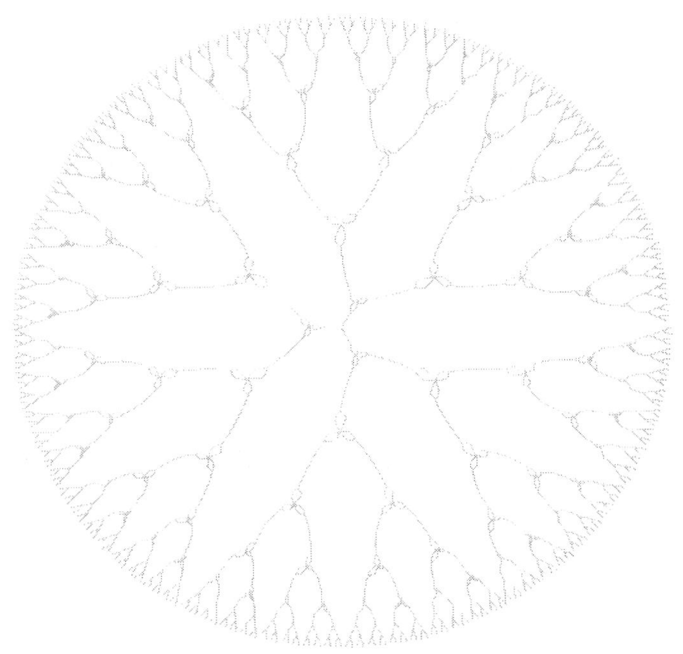

Advance Praise

"*Your Sacred Wealth Code* goes far beyond applying spiritual principles to charting what can be an elusive path to prosperity. Prema Lee Gurreri not only describes a conscious path to freedom and wealth, she also asks the penetrating questions to reveal what wealth means to you personally and the beliefs and cultural messages that stand in your way. Prepare to do some soul searching with this beautiful book as you align internally with the expansion you—and your soul—want you to experience in all areas of your life: money, energy, love and time."

- GAIL LARSEN, best-selling author of *Transformational Speaking: If You Want to Change the World, Tell a Better Story*

"Having worked personally with Prema, I know her intuitive and healing capacity firsthand. She is the real deal, and in her book, *Your Sacred Wealth Code*, she takes her extensive personal and professional experience and distills it into a powerful framework for accessing and activating your true wealth—a wealth that is not just about having more than enough money, but about attracting more than enough of everything you need to live an amazing, meaningful life. As you read and apply the wisdom in this book, you will be turning on the divine power plant within you that can provide everything you need, want, hope for, and desire in an ever-expanding, never-ending flow of prosperity. So, read this book! Unlock your Wealth Code, and live the life you were truly meant to live!"

- DEREK RYDALL, best-selling author of *Emergence*, host of the top podcast, "Emergence"

"Prema takes us on a journey in this beautiful and wise book, *Your Sacred Wealth Code* that has never been presented before. This is easily one of the most practical and enlightening journeys to real wealth, with a definitely personal twist. Prema has helped thousands discover their passion and purpose, and channel that into true and permanent wealth. This is a can't-miss book that may not only change *your* world but will change *the* world. Prema walks her talk, and is a true leader in wealth consciousness on the planet at this time."

- DR. KIMBERLY McGEORGE, ND, CNH, energy healer, remote viewer radio host of "Secret to Everything" on The X Zone, founder of SecretToEverything.com

"Thank you, Prema, for sharing your conscious wealth wisdom! We loved that you identified wealth as more than materialism, including spiritual and emotional wealth. You have put together a well-written, effective and eye-opening book that helps the reader identify where they may be blocking their own abundance. We certainly feel ready and able to allow and create more wealth after reading!"

- TAMARA VEITCH DeFAZIO & RENE DeFAZIO, authors of *One Great Year* and the *Great Year* Series

"I'm in awe. This is the most revealing, empowering, and inspiring book I've seen on attracting wealth from your own unique sacred path. Read it. Live it. Prosper from it."

- DR. JOE VITALE, author of *The Attractor Factor*, star of *The Secret*

"The way we have been taught to think about wealth and money is too narrow; it doesn't serve us anymore. If you're passionate about growing a life and business that is totally in sync with you, your purpose, your passion, and your mission in the world, *Your Sacred Wealth Code* is the key to your success. It goes beyond strategy to the core of what makes us tick as wealth attractors. I highly recommend this book!"

- BRET GREGORY, author of *Attract Customers Now From Facebook: Simple, Cost-Effective Marketing For Entrepreneurs*

"*Your Sacred Wealth Code* lays out a transformational path for aligning with your purpose so 'wealth springs like a fountain.' It will open your eyes to how we limit ourselves when we think of wealth as being exclusively about money. And best of all, it will show you once and for all that you can't have true wealth without living your purpose … and how to discover exactly what your purpose is. I highly recommend this wise and compassionate road map for finally sharing your deepest gifts with the world, and receiving all the gifts the world has in store for you."

-JENNIFER CORNBLEET, success coach, best-selling author of *Raw Food Made Easy*, founder of TastyLifeCoaching.com

"There are people in this world who are extraordinarily gifted, and Prema Lee Gurreri is one of those people. In her latest book, *Your Sacred Wealth Code; Unlock Your Soul Blueprint For Purpose and Prosperity*, Prema brilliantly presents a well a written playbook full of stories, questions, and exercises that take the reader on a journey of inner wisdom. The more one delves into the book, the more the path becomes illuminated, leading to joyous discovery of purpose and its connection to wealth as it relates to one's relationships, career, business, finances and more. I love this book and Prema's insights. Its time has come."

-TERRY WILDEMANN, CEC, CPCC, CPBA
professional speaker, certified Success Coach, author

"Everyone has wealth locked inside of them. The key is uncovering what is stopping you from achieving it. Prema's book demonstrates how you can easily apply the truth of wealth to your life based on who you already are! As a Global Brand Visionary and Empowerment Coach for women leaders, I feel that this work is needed in the world; I highly recommend this book to everyone struggling to master wealth in their lives!"

-HEATHER PICKEN, best-selling author of *Woman On Fire*
entrepreneur, founder of www.HeatherPicken.com

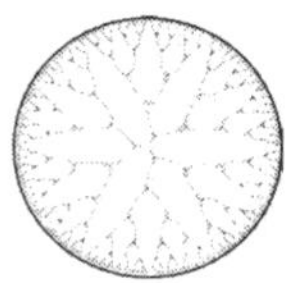

Table of Contents

Exercises & Media

Exercises marked with ** can also be downloaded in audio format at www.SacredWealthCode.com/book

Find even more interactive materials and extra content in the Resources section on page 267!

Your Sacred Wealth Code

UNLOCK YOUR SOUL BLUEPRINT FOR
PURPOSE & PROSPERITY

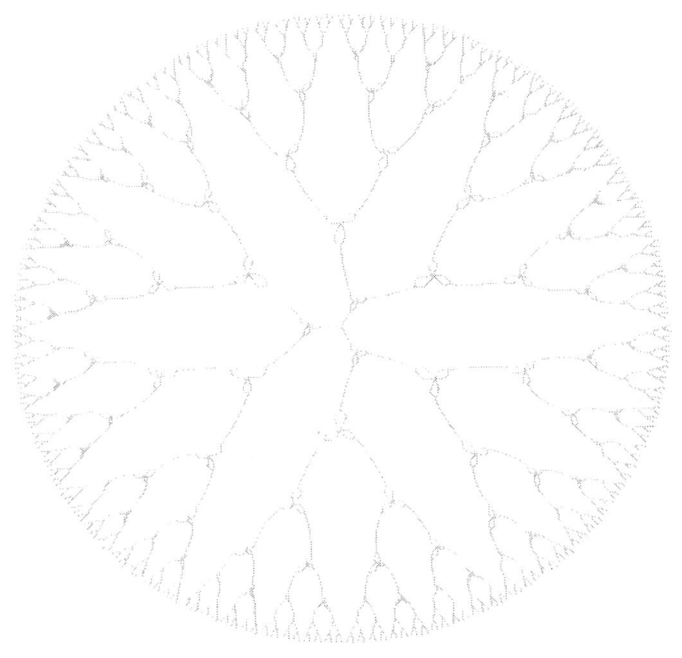

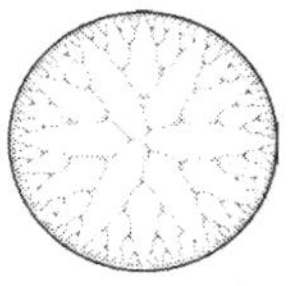

Introduction

WHAT TO EXPECT

Be who you are, do what you love, and live a wealthy life.

What if it actually *is* that simple?
It can be, if you are living from your Sacred Wealth Code!

We all have a desire for wealth and prosperity. But there's a deeper meaning to this desire than simply accumulating material goods or fattening our bank accounts. When properly aligned with our purpose, passion, and high-value gifts, our desire for wealth and prosperity is like a compass pointing us toward our greater purpose in the world. By actualizing our true wealth dreams, we can live on purpose and serve the world at large—all at the same time!

You have a unique design and internal formula for attracting wealth. This formula is encoded in your soul blueprint—and like your fingerprints, that encoding is unlike that of any other human being. It's written in the universal language of purpose and prosperity, and it's called your Sacred Wealth Code.

According to your soul, wealth is whatever you need—materially, emotionally, and spiritually—to fulfill your purpose on Earth. This is the concept of wealth we will explore in this book, and the seed which will blossom into true wealth for you through this work.

So, right here, right now, embrace your soul's desire for wealth and prosperity, and know that, once you step into alignment with your soul blueprint for wealth, you will be empowered to actualize your purpose and greater calling in the world. You will get to know the what, how, and why of your reality as it relates to purpose and prosperity. You will learn to move beyond the activities you are simply good at, and wield your high-value gifts like the superpowers they are. Most of all, you will be called to grow beyond your comfort zone, the status quo, and the inner programming that's been keeping you stuck, and embrace your highest potential.

I teach the Sacred Wealth Code to entrepreneurs, leaders, and change agents who want to align with the wealth that they know, on a deep, soul level, they have the power to manifest for themselves. Through this body of work, and using the tools in this book, you too can discover, as I and so many of my clients have, that internal "home base" where prosperity and purpose intersect, and from which wealth springs like a fountain.

If you are willing to undertake a quest to discover your soul blueprint; if you are willing to accept the challenges with the successes, and let them inform you; if you are willing to drop down into the core of who you are and listen to what your soul is telling you about your wealth dream and its promise for your life, you are in the right place.

Your Sacred Wealth Code is waiting.

Are you ready to reveal it?

HOW TO USE THIS BOOK

This book is a guide, playbook, and journal all in one. It provides you with everything you need to discover, understand, embody, and operate from your Sacred Wealth Code to manifest your wealth vision and create a life of purpose and prosperity. It's an experiential process that will lead you deep into the realm of your soul, and discover how your purpose, passion, gifts, and challenges all contribute to why, how, and through what channels you are uniquely designed to create wealth.

Through information, stories, meditations, and experiential Wealth Focus practices, you will undertake a journey to discover your soul's blueprint and reveal your personal Sacred Wealth Code. There is writing space at the end of each chapter to help you engage fully with the questions and exercises presented. It is important to journal about what you discover along your journey, as each chapter and step builds on the one before.

In the Resources section at the back of the book, you will find links to access free audio and video versions of the processes, exercises, and meditations in this book, so you can engage with the work in the way that best suits your learning style.

Regardless of how you choose to engage with these processes, the awareness and skills you gain as you work through them will eventually become a way of life, and help you create wealth that flows to you in an inspired and easeful way.

Unlike many wealth creation systems, this is an "inside out" process which asks you to engage with the truth of who you are in order to blaze a path to the wealth you desire. You won't find business tips, investment strategies, or other such instruction in this book. Instead, you'll learn, through reflection and practice, how to identify and execute your own strategy of inspired action which is uniquely tailored to your soul's path and your high-value gifts.

How you choose to undertake the journey to your Sacred Wealth Code is completely up to you. You can go through this as a solo journey, or invite a friend to do it with you. You can work on a chapter a week, or read the whole book from start to finish and then go back to the beginning to work through the exercises with full knowledge of where you're headed.

Whatever approach you choose, know that you are on a collision course with your own greatness. I'm so excited for you to align with the best of yourself, create your wealth dream, and revel in the free and fulfilled life you've always desired.

With love,
Prema

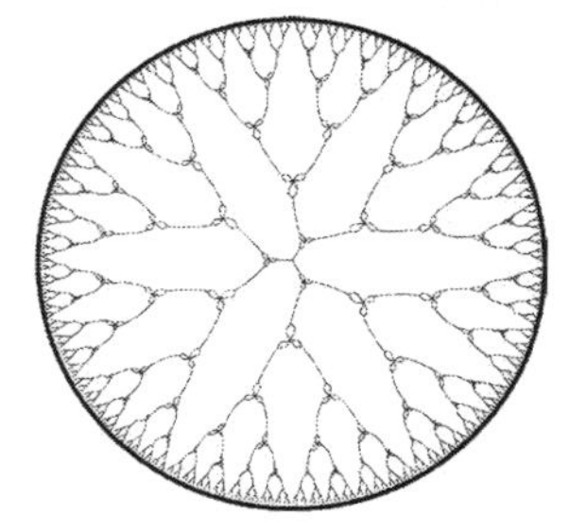

Part I

WHAT IS WEALTH?

What Is Wealth?

In order to create wealth, you need to know what wealth actually means to you. More, you need to be aligned with wealth according to your own personal definition.

Wealth, in broad terms, is everything you need to fulfill your greatest purpose here on Earth. It includes money, time, freedom, security, self-expression, and any other energy which contributes to your personal fulfillment and your soul's greatest expression.

Therefore, wealth to you might mean material possessions: a beautiful home, a nice car, a fat bank account. It might mean travel, freedom, and complete influence over your own time. Or, it might mean an abundance of stability and certainty in the form of relationships, steady work, and a well-planned future. Whatever your definition of wealth, we will explore it and use the knowledge to delve deeper into your wealth dream—and by extension, your greater purpose in this lifetime.

Your personal definition of wealth is vital to uncovering your Sacred Wealth Code because your desire for wealth is a natural part of your human construction, and one of many keys to your soul's truth.

Before we can identify and work with your soul blueprint for wealth—your Sacred Wealth Code—we first need to identify three things:

1. Your current relationship to wealth,
2. Your current beliefs about wealth and your capacity to achieve it, and
3. How your current path is (and is not) supporting your unique wealth dream and wealth alignment.

Once you learn what wealth actually means to you, why you desire it, and what is holding you back from attracting it, you can create a purposeful plan to navigate to the intersection of purpose and prosperity within your soul where your Sacred Wealth Code lives.

Let's get started.

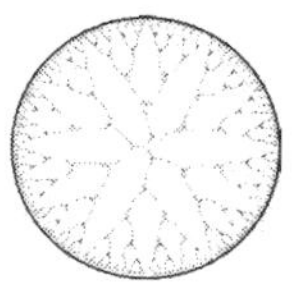

Chapter One

A HIGHER MEANING FOR WEALTH

When I was eighteen, I bought an old Volkswagen camper van. With my new home-on-wheels, a few thousand dollars in my savings account, and some camping supplies, I quit my two jobs and set off on the road-tripping adventure of a lifetime.

I didn't have a lot of stuff, but I had time, and I was free to roam. I knew I could find a job any time I needed one, and that I would always find a way to get what I needed to fuel the next stage of my grand adventure. The world was my oyster. I felt wealthy beyond measure.

As I've grown older, my definition of wealth has evolved. Freedom is still of very high importance to me, and when I know I can give myself and my family the kinds of experiences I desire, I feel wealthy. I also have a beautiful home, and the resources to contribute to my children's lives in any way I choose.

Most of all, I feel wealthy when I can use my abundance to contribute to my purpose and mission in the world, and create a movement. Through connections with other people, technology, and the wise application of financial resources, I can effectively use the gifts I've been given in my soul blueprint, and contribute to the betterment of humanity.

In other words, my wealth is more than dollars and cents. It is a tool which enables the fulfillment of my purpose on Earth.

WEALTH IS MORE THAN MONEY

Wealth is everything we need—materially, spiritually, and emotionally—in order to fulfill our purpose on Earth. It is the accumulation of everything we need, want, and desire.

More, wealth is the *perception* and *belief* that we have everything we need, want, and desire. In order to *be* wealthy, we have to *feel* wealthy. Otherwise, we just have a lot of stuff.

This is a higher meaning of wealth than the one we usually encounter. Or, depending on your perspective, it might be a foundational meaning. After all, what we see as wealth in others' lives is really only the superficial trappings. We can't see how they *feel*, or how they are living their purpose, until we look deeper.

Often, we equate wealth solely to money, but that's actually inaccurate. Money is simply the common energy of exchange in our world—the unit of measurement by which we value the intangible resources of time, energy, security, relationships, love, and freedom.

I think it's safe to say that everyone, from every walk of life, wants to be wealthy. It's a desire that we are born with, and one that we nurture as we grow. After all, I don't know anyone who spends their time asking, "How can I be poorer? How can I have more lack in my life?" Do you?

Your Concept of Wealth

When you think of being "wealthy," what does that look like to you? Is it a numerical benchmark, like, "I'll be wealthy when I have a million dollars in the bank"? Or is wealth more of a feeling to you, a state of being, a new and upgraded operating platform? What resources, relationships, and mindsets do you need to attract in order to live in wealth and abundance?

Wealth is very personal. It's different for each of us. Once you know what wealth actually looks and feels like to you, you will be more able to attract it.

Another question to ask yourself is, "*Why* do I want to be wealthy?" Why do you want more money? What do you think money will allow you to do, be, and create?

Here are just a few reasons that people desire to create wealth. Perhaps some of them also apply to you.

I want to be wealthy because ...

- I want greater security.
- I want to buy a new home (or car, boat, camper, etc.).
- I want to travel and experience the world.
- I want to create a healthier lifestyle without worrying about the price tag.
- I want to start a business.
- I want to create or assist a charity.
- I want to leave a legacy for my children and grandchildren.
- I want to live as an example to others.
- I want to start a movement.

As you explore the question of "why," try not to judge yourself. There are no wrong reasons to desire wealth.

Our why = our purpose. *Why* you desire is actually more important than *what* you desire.

Whatever makes you feel wealthy is important, because it gives you a clue as to your deeper motivations, values, and purpose. For example, if you want wealth because it will increase your prestige and visibility, it's not something to be ashamed of. In fact, these attributes are probably tied to your greater purpose.

When you know and acknowledge your "big why" around wealth, you actually open up avenues for greater wealth to come to you. You open up pathways, make connections, and see possibilities everywhere, and are more likely to take action to acquire the resources you need to move forward.

We live in an ever-expanding universe. Our desire for wealth is extremely personal, but it's also part of that collective expansion energy. When we tap into that truth, and understand that our desire for wealth is innately connected to our purpose in life, we invite the universe to work on our behalf.

My grandmother, the matriarch of our family, was a seamstress. She came from poverty, but she had a strong will, and knew that there was always a way to get what she wanted.

She worked hard. *Really* hard. She sewed for a factory from the age of twelve. Her wages were not enough to make ends meet, never mind to create the life she dreamed about, so she sewed for a lot of people on the side, and took odd jobs whenever the opportunity arose. Opportunities seemed to magically appear for her whenever she needed them. Her "regular" job did not provide her with security, but she created that security for herself through investments, stocks, and good planning. She had money stashed everywhere—under the mattress, in the cupboards, in safe deposit boxes. Knowing she had access to money from multiple sources at all times made her feel wealthy and secure.

By the time she was ready to retire, she was able to live off of her investments. Whenever anyone in the family needed a loan or financial advice, they came to Grandma. She created all kinds of experiences for herself and her family that many people never get to enjoy—like traveling around the world. She was driven by her purpose to do her best to create the best life possible for herself and her family.

By society's standards, my grandmother wasn't "rich." In fact, for most of her life, she was barely middle-class. She lived in a tiny apartment, and wore clothes that she'd made herself. She wasn't extravagant, or ostentatious—but in her mind, she was wealthy. She had created everything she needed to do the things that mattered to her.

On the other hand, many people have a ton of money, but never feel wealthy. I know millionaires who started to feel poor because they lost some money in the stock market, or because the value of their real estate investments dropped a few percentage points. Despite all the zeroes in their bank balances, these individuals were no longer wealthy, because they no longer believed that they were supported, empowered, and free to choose the path that was most aligned with their purpose.

THE INTERSECTION OF WEALTH & PURPOSE

Although wealth is the acquisition of whatever you need to fulfill your purpose, you don't need to fully understand your purpose in order to be, and feel, wealthy.

Yes, it seems like a paradox—but the truth is, there are multiple levels of purpose. In some way, we are connected to all of them, whether we are aware of it or not. Part of my intention for this book is that you gain more clarity around your purpose, your high-value gifts, and your deepest desires for your life, so that you can attract wealth with greater precision and clarity.

As we discovered in the last section, our desire for wealth is more than just a desire for *more*—although society often portrays it that way. **When we reel our desire back to its essence and energy, we see that desire is a trigger.** It pushes us to reach beyond our comfort zone: to grow, to imagine, to create. This energy directly contributes to the expansion of our selves, our personal sphere of influence, our planet, and the universe as a whole.

Remember, wealth is what we need to fulfill our purpose. And since our desire points the way to our purpose and triggers our actions in that direction, our desire for wealth is a major key to unlocking our greatest gifts and talents and living the most amazing possible life. This is the truth at the heart of the Sacred Wealth Code, which I'll expand upon in the next section.

It's natural to desire wealth because wealth (*your* definition of it) is inherent in your soul blueprint. We all have a place in our soul blueprint dedicated to our purpose and vision. Wealth, and our desire for it, is the means by which we are empowered to express those things.

Consciously, subconsciously, and unconsciously, you know that the beacon of your desire for abundance is important, so you attend to it constantly. Maybe you're not fully aware of this fire-stoking; maybe you simply have a feeling that you are more than your current circumstances, and that you are meant for greater things. The good news is, you get to decide what that "more" is. You get to decide what wealth and abundance mean to you.

So, right here, right now, I ask you to embrace your desire for wealth and prosperity. Know that, when properly aligned, it will empower you to actualize your purpose in the world. It will call you to continue to grow beyond your comfort zone and the status quo, and evolve into your highest potential.

When you are actualizing wealth on your own terms, based on your own definition of "wealthiness," you are working for the greater good of yourself, the planet, and humanity.

For many of us, this runs counter to what we were told about money and wealth as children. Perhaps we learned that wanting more money is "greedy," or that a person can only get rich by trampling others. If you have old programming along those lines, I encourage you to set it aside for the remainder of the time you spend with this book. Such untruths will only leave you second-guessing your purpose, and the desires that can guide you there.

Just for a moment, imagine a world where everyone was connected with their truest, most authentic definition of wealth. Imagine that every person was fully aligned with their desire to expand, and that each had everything they needed to fulfill their greater purpose. Imagine how different the world would be, and the enormous contributions that each person could make. Wouldn't it be amazing?

I've always known, deep in my bones, that wealth would give me freedom. That freedom has looked different at various points throughout my lifetime, but it's always given me a sense of empowerment and lightness. I want to be free, because when I am free I am purposeful. When I am purposeful, I am powerful, and when I am powerful, I am creating a soul-satisfying life.

You have an important reason why you want to be wealthy. **Wealth is what you need to fulfill your purpose, so your why for wealth = the key to your purpose.** Your why is the trigger for you to show up and shine as your best self, which will align you with wealth. *You* get to decide what wealth means to you, and what you need to acquire to fulfill your greater purpose and live your soul-satisfying life.

WEALTH CONSCIOUSNESS & YOUR SACRED WEALTH CODE

I've always had the gift of intuition. It is part of what led me to Yoga and Vedic Astrology, the two life sciences which became the first vehicles through which I could fully express my high-value gifts to connect with and empower others.

Vedic Astrology is an ancient system which is derived from the Vedas, the most ancient of Hindu scriptures. While some practitioners use it primarily for prediction, I was driven to tap into Vedic Astrology to help people understand how their patterns, choices, and purpose are encoded at a soul level, and teach them how to align with the most positive aspects of their inherent personal makeup.

After years of exploring Vedic Astrology as both art and science, I began to ask, "How can I express the wisdom of Vedic Astrology in a format and terminology that's easier for people to understand?" The Sacred Wealth Code was my answer. It was downloaded, in a way, appearing not just as a response to my question but as a universal language with unlimited potential to help human beings unlock their soul paths and live with greater prosperity, purpose, connection, and joy.

It also appeared precisely at the time when I needed it most.

I've always been interested in finding the intersection between prosperity and purpose for myself and my service to others—an alignment known as *dhana yogas* in Vedic Astrology—but for many years I struggled to find my financial "sweet spot."

Before I aligned with my personal Sacred Wealth Code, I had a yoga and healing arts center where I taught yoga, offered Vedic Astrology readings, trained yoga teachers, and worked with people on a very intimate and personal level. My space, called Yoga and Beyond, was an umbrella under which I could teach and integrate all that I knew about the practical and spiritual aspects of yoga, astrology, and soul purpose.

In the five years that I owned it, Yoga and Beyond blossomed into a world-class yoga center and thriving community. It was a big investment: I had two studios, highly-trained teachers, healing practitioners, desk staff, retail space, you name it. I poured my heart and soul into the place, and for a long time, I really felt like I was living my purpose there, and using my gifts in the most positive way possible. I was touching lives, creating community, helping others to live on purpose, and helping people from all walks of life discover how to integrate the spiritual into the practical in their everyday lives, which I call "living from the inside out."

But something was amiss. My business was doing six figures in sales, but I was taking very little money home at the end of the week. I was deeply in debt, and struggled to balance my time between teaching classes, seeing private clients, masterminding the business, and managing the everyday operations.

Then, my marriage fell apart—and my already-struggling financial world crumbled with it. Things grew increasingly more difficult, both at home and at the yoga center. And, in the midst of it all, I realized a profound truth that would totally shake up my life and shift my financial reality.

Throughout my business journey, I had been using many of my valuable skills, such as organizing, facilitating, and managing my business. But I hadn't been focused on my high-value gifts—my *dhana yogas*, the energies which exist in that sweet spot where purpose and prosperity meet.

In other words, I wasn't fully aligned with my soul's natural blueprint for wealth, prosperity, ease, and joy. And I had to do the work to rectify that if I was ever going to dig myself out of the hole I'd fallen into.

I started on a practical level, reaching out to ask for help with my business. I envisioned someone coming in as a partner or investor to level the scales again, but I had already moved too far out of balance. I searched, planned, and even pleaded, but I couldn't right my ship.

Finally, deep in the dark night of my soul, and with nowhere to turn, I realized that I had to let the center go. I had to surrender fully, and find peace around something that my mind wanted to label as "failure." It was a rough road, and got even rockier when I ran into some challenges with getting out of the last few months of my lease. I was literally brought to my knees before it was all over.

And then, with nothing left to hold on to, I was finally brought face to face with my reality. I needed to do the deep, spiritual work to uncover why I had created this reality for myself. I needed to pull myself out of whatever shadow I was living in. And I needed to ask for help.

Asking for help was one of the most difficult things I've ever done. I've always been self-reliant and independent, and part of my definition of freedom was "not owing anyone anything." But, after a lot of prayer and self-reflection, I put the word out there to my community that I needed help to stay in business.

In a week's time, I was gifted with $10,000 from multiple donors. They arrived alongside a stack of cards that still make me cry every time I read them. "Thank you for giving me the opportunity to help you," they read.

This was a deep, spiritual lesson for me: I didn't have to do it all alone to be valuable. It was okay to ask for help, and I was worthy of being helped. More, the offer of assistance could be a blessing for the giver. Generosity benefits both parties equally.

Although the physical location for my yoga center was gone, my business wasn't. I simply needed to shift gears. I went into private practice, and was soon offered a gorgeous home on twelve acres which had space for a private studio. It was basically like a retreat center, only I would be living there!

In these new surroundings, gifted by the support of so many, I made a commitment to align with—and stay connected to—my highest potential and my high-value gifts. No longer could I waste my time and precious life force doing what I was merely good at. I needed to do what I was uniquely *great* at, and deliver it as an offering to the world.

It was then that the Sacred Wealth Code truly revealed itself to me. I saw clearly, for the first time, what my personal Wealth Code truly was, and how I could follow it to create the purposeful, fulfilling life I desired.

I realized that we all have a unique blueprint for prosperity, and that it can be revealed to us through Vedic Astrology. The structure of our soul blueprint is composed of our *yogas*—the alignments of archetypal energetic forces within our natal charts. The ways in which these archetypal forces interact with one another reveal our *dhana yogas*: the places where prosperity and purpose intersect. Our secret formula for wealth and prosperity is literally written for us at the time of our birth!

This is the Sacred Wealth Code: the universal language of purpose and prosperity. Being a sacred language, it is also an archetypal language, with each of the Sacred Wealth Archetypes revealing itself as one face of a planetary energy. (You'll get to know the Sacred Wealth Archetypes in detail later in this book.) While not all of us are wired to intuitively understand Sanskrit and the esoteric language of the Vedas, the Archetypes are universal, and translate across the boundaries of age, faith, training, time, and experience.

As I started to clue in to the Sacred Wealth Archetypes and how they relate to one another within each individual's soul blueprint, I was able to help people integrate and embody their innate gifts and wisdom in much more powerful ways. Why?

Because by understanding the Archetypes which underpin our personal Sacred Wealth Code, we can also understand the what, how, and why of our reality, and take the steps we need to fully align with our soul's path.

Engaging with this new body of work also prompted some intense self-reflection for me. For a long time, I realized, I had been stuck in the shadow side of my Wealth Code, living just off-center from where I was really meant to be. More, I had been using many of my innate and acquired skills—mostly around administration and organization—but putting those skills at the forefront of my work and trying to run the business by myself left me feeling tapped out and disconnected. In that space, I simply didn't have the bandwidth or energy to operate at my highest potential, or fully connect with my high-value gifts. This vicious cycle had kept me unfulfilled and broke for years.

Radiant with this new knowledge, I started an online business centered around my work with the Sacred Wealth Code. Within six months, I was able to double, then triple, my rates, and reach a global community as well as my local one.

Now, I work with men and women from around the world to tap into the promise of their Sacred Wealth Code, realign with their high-value gifts, and live lives of purpose, passion, and prosperity.

Looking back, I could say that my yoga center failed, but I don't see it that way. Yoga and Beyond was a beautiful landmark on my soul's path, and it helped me turn the corner and uncover the necessary knowledge to align with my true nature and receive the body of work that I am now sharing with you. I needed to live the truth of my own Sacred Wealth Code, and integrate it fully, in order for it to come through me in a way that could serve others.

If you are ready to start living your own wealth truth, you need to begin by understanding your dreams for, and connection to, wealth. These Wealth Focus exercises will get you started.

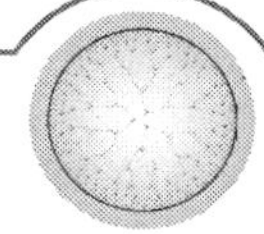

Wealth Focus

Part of the reason the Sacred Wealth Code works so well is that it brings things down to a practical—and therefore, *useful*—level. Information is only powerful if it can be integrated.

That's why, in each chapter of this book, you will find Wealth Focus exercises to help you integrate the information I've presented in a practical and actionable way.

As a way to focus on and assimilate the information I've presented in this chapter, take some time to answer the following questions. You can write in a journal or on your computer, or make a voice recording using your smart device. Whatever method you prefer, be sure to keep a record of all of your answers, so you can revisit them later and chart your progress.

Reflection

When you hear the word "wealth," what visions come to mind?

____

____

____

____

____

____

What wealth do you desire to create for yourself?

Why do you want this wealth?

When you have wealth, what will be possible for you?

When you have wealth, what will you make possible for others?

How do you hold yourself back from receiving wealth?

Where have you been selling yourself short, or actively repelling wealth?

Action Steps

Write (or speak) for at least fifteen minutes about your vision of a wealthy life. Get really imaginative, and be specific. Be sure to touch on the following points in your narrative:

- What would a day in your wealthy life look like?
- How will you feel?
- What will you do differently than you are doing now in your life, your business, and your community?
- How will you use your wealth to support your greater purpose (as you currently understand it)?

My Wealth Vision Statement

____

____

____

____

____

____

____

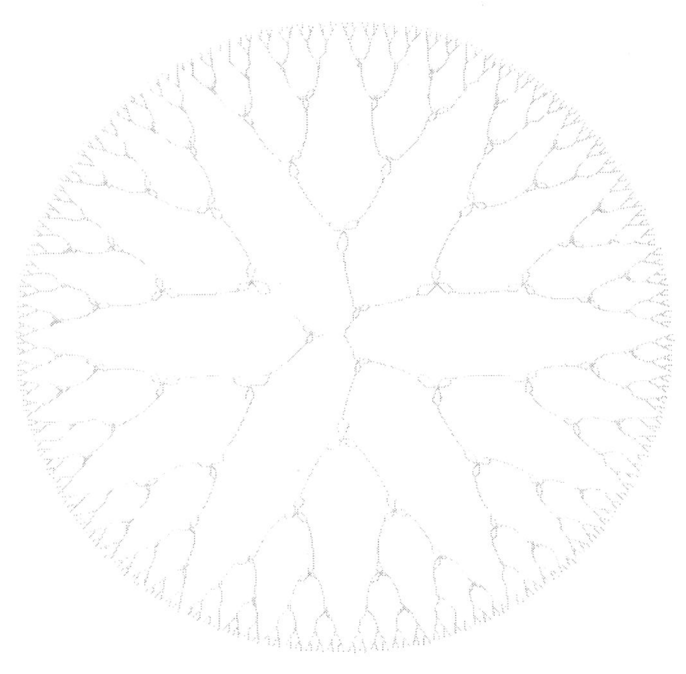

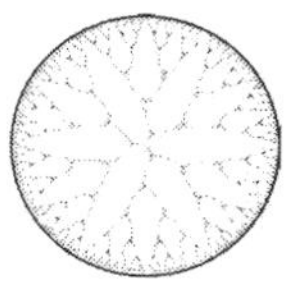

Chapter Two

YOU ARE UNIQUELY DESIGNED FOR WEALTH

In order to *have* wealth, you must be *aligned with* wealth.

We are born with this soul alignment for wealth. It's written into our beings at the time of our birth. However, our early experiences and the programming we receive from our parents, family, friends, the media, and society messes up this alignment, and by the time we are seven years old (the age by which most of our beliefs are programmed into our subconscious minds) we are no longer fully in touch with our birthright and our personal Sacred Wealth Code.

If we are aware enough, and curious enough, we often recognize this misalignment somewhere in our adulthood. We wonder what's wrong with us, and why we can't have the wealth that others have. We justify our current lack of wealth, saying things like, "Some people are just born rich," or "I guess I'm destined to be poor." Or, we treat our lack of wealth as a personal failing, believing that if we only do more, work harder, and sacrifice more, we can rise above our current mediocrity.

We try various means to get aligned with our wealth—following the formulas of money gurus, engaging in risky business ventures, and even playing the lottery. Most of the time, these strategies fail. Why? Because they're attempting to fix an internal problem with an external solution!

There is really only one way that we can find our "sweet spot" for wealth, and that's to work from the inside out, align with our soul blueprint, and live from the place where our purpose and prosperity meet.

When you discover your Sacred Wealth Code and do the inner work necessary to align with it, you will naturally draw more wealth toward you, and in ways you never would have expected.

THE INNER PATH TO YOUR SACRED WEALTH CODE

The belief that only some people are destined to be wealthy, while others are destined to be poor, is simply untrue.

When I look at my clients' Sacred Wealth Codes, I do see that some people are encoded to acquire wealth from their ancestry and family lineage. However, accessing ancestral wealth is only one of the many paths open to them to create wealth in their lives, and sitting around and waiting for an inheritance isn't exactly a sound strategy for wealth creation!

I have seen other clients whose Sacred Wealth Codes contain none of the "fated" wealth points (like ancestral acquisition or lucky windfalls) create wealth beyond their wildest dreams simply by working in alignment with their soul blueprints and erasing the subconscious programming that was holding them back.

Another common belief around wealth is that you have to work really, *really* hard to get it. Hard work is a pathway that can create wealth to a certain extent, for certain people. But for many of us, it actually holds us back. It keeps us busy with task after task when our high-value gifts lie elsewhere.

Now, not working "hard" doesn't equal being lazy. I personally can—and do—work long hours at times. But while I'm working, I also forget that I'm working, because I love what I'm doing so much and feel so inspired by my work. During these times, I'm accomplishing a lot—but am I "working hard"? I don't think so. I'm simply putting time and energy toward the tasks and activities that fulfill my desires and my purpose. I'm soul-driven.

Working hard, to me, is pushing through to complete tasks that aren't necessarily fulfilling or rewarding, just to say that they're done. Working hard is doing it myself when I should be delegating, or spending time utilizing my less-valuable gifts just so I can tick an item off my to-do list.

This is a new mode of operation for me. Growing up, money was never just given to me, and as a result I developed a strong work ethic. I also developed a belief that I had to work really hard to get money. And since money meant freedom to me, I felt that I had to work *really* hard to be free.

I would work twelve- to sixteen-hour days for months at a time, then take a travel break to enjoy the freedom I had earned. I worked full-time and then some, in jobs ranging from chef to organizational manager to personal growth specialist. I spent a lot of frustrating years that way. It felt like I could never work hard enough to earn the freedom I wanted, and that constant striving diminished my self-value.

When I stepped full-time into doing what I love, on purpose—and started making a good, a great, and finally an *exceptional* living at it—I realized that I didn't have to earn my freedom through hard work. I was already wired to experience freedom, because it was written into my Sacred Wealth Code. All I had to do was to step into the alignment of my passion and purpose, and freedom was waiting there for me.

The people I work with to reveal their Sacred Wealth Codes come to understand, deep in their hearts, that there is a way for them to become wealthy doing what they love and are drawn to, instead of what they "have" to do. Whether it's art, music, healing, coaching, activism, problem-solving, or something else, they see pathways to abundance at every junction of their passion and purpose. They were able to see past the lie that you can't make money doing what you love, and now consistently find ways to align their high-value gifts with their vision for themselves and their lives.

So, ask yourself: "What can I pour my energy, love, time, and passion into?" What activities are you happy to get lost in? What could you do all day, every day, for the next five, ten, or twenty years?

The magic of your Sacred Wealth Code is that when you align your passion, purpose, and high-value gifts, and live true to what you love, you will automatically attract wealth! When you are living on purpose, and giving 100 percent of your energy and dedication to that purpose, the universe will support you with everything you need to live the way you need to live, feel the way you want to feel, contribute the way you want to contribute, and collaborate the way you want to collaborate.

This is why it's so important to understand the wealth that you actually want—and the reason why, in the Wealth Focus section of the last chapter, you identified what wealth actually means to you. As I've stated before, wealth is unique to each of us, and we are *all* wired for wealth in our own way. Everyone has a "magic number," a dollar amount, a car, a home, a lifestyle, something that sets the benchmark for wealth in our minds. And what you receive when you live from that intersection of purpose and prosperity is exactly reflective of your ideas about wealth.

Which brings us to our third limiting belief about wealth: that there is only so much to go around.

There are many variations within this belief system. Here are just a few that might be rolling around in your subconscious mind:

- Money is the root of all evil
- If you want more money, you're greedy
- It takes money to make money
- If I have money, others won't be able to receive what they need
- You have to spend less to have more

We live in an infinite and ever-expanding universe. Our desires to create, to manifest, and to receive are part of this expansion. Remember, money is energy, and in an endlessly-expanding universe, there is an endless supply of energy from which to create.

This isn't magical thinking. It's quantum physics. Science is proving these statements more definitively every day. And, if it's true that we live in an expanding universe, why can't wealth expand as well?

When you are living on purpose, the universe has your back. But if your ideas about wealth don't reflect, or allow for, the wealth you want to receive—or *need* to receive—to live your purpose, things can get stuck really fast. Ditto if you feel guilty or insecure about receiving wealth for expressing your purpose through your work.

So, ask yourself, right now: "Is what I believe about wealth actually true?"

If you're not sure, use the following Wealth Focus exercise on the following page to clarify and hone in on how your beliefs about money are affecting your ability to connect with your wealth and wealth dream.

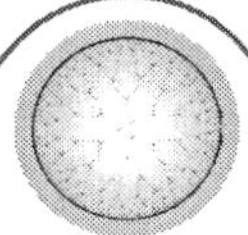

Wealth Focus

Reflection

Make a list of beliefs that you hold around money. What words or sayings echo in your head every time you think or talk about money?

1 ____

2 ____

3 ____

4 ____

5 ____

6 ____

7 ____

8 ____

9 ____

10 _______________________________________

Next, write out everything you can identify about what's blocking you from receiving the wealth you desire.

____

____

____

____

____

Chances are, you will see some clear overlap between what you believe about money and what's true in your life!

Now, circle the top three beliefs or circumstances that you feel are blocking you the most right now. Apply the process below to each of the three.

Action Steps

1 Take a few deep breaths to get centered.

2 Take responsibility for what you believe, and what those beliefs have created. Say, "I am creating what I am experiencing by believing ____."

3 Ask yourself, "Is what I am telling myself about _____ actually true?" If the answer is yes, what proof do you have? Go back and ask again until you find out what's underneath the belief.

4 Ask yourself, "What is a more empowered choice I can make around this situation?" Write your answer below.

____

____

____

____

____

____

5 Make a plan of action around your empowered choice and execute it within twenty-four hours.

____

____

____

____

____

____

____

THE ENERGY OF MONEY

Here's a question for you:

Why do we make wealth all about money?

Money is a form of energy, just like love, time, and breath. However, in our modern world, we have made money the most common currency of exchange. It's everywhere. We trade our time, our labor—and even, sadly, our love—for it. If you look around your home, most of what you will see are things that have been purchased, or that money has been exchanged for.

Right now, I'm looking around my office. My desk, my computer, my vase and the flowers in it: all these things have been purchased with money.

Without money, we can't easily obtain the things we need to live. That's why our money stuff hits us so painfully. It's a matter of survival. That, combined with the misconceptions and limiting beliefs about money that we pick up from our parents, family, friends, society, and early experiences, can really jam up our energy around money, and make it hard to access—and be guided by—our Sacred Wealth Code and our soul blueprint for wealth.

When our internal Wealth Code circuits are jammed, it makes it hard for us to create, receive, and flow with money. All of those misconceptions and limiting beliefs are playing subliminally in the background, and keeping the wealth we really want at arm's length. We might be working really hard to create wealth, but while this "white noise" is buzzing in our ears, we won't realize the full results of our efforts.

Here's the thing: money, wealth, and spirituality are inextricably connected. Using spiritual tools to work on your money stuff can be one of the most challenging, and most rewarding, processes you can undertake, because your beliefs about money, worth, and value touch every area of your life.

When I had to let go of my yoga center, I was taken to my knees. To get through this dark night of the soul, I deepened my study of Vedic Astrology and meditated on what I knew and believed about the laws of the universe. I wanted to understand my soul blueprint and its relationship to the energy of wealth and abundance. This potent self-inquiry enabled me to drill down into the essence of my beliefs about myself and how I related to money and wealth. When I discovered how I was living out of sync with my purpose and prosperity, I was able to course-correct and get back on my path. Soon, I was not only attracting wealth and clients, but I also felt happier, freer, and more aligned with my own truth.

When your soul speaks—when your truth speaks—it can transform fear on the spot. But until you get to that deep, spiritual place where the truth can be heard, you will still have to contend with all of the noise of your false beliefs. That's why inner work is as vital to wealth as physical work.

Your Wealth Operating Instructions

You have a personal "Wealth User's Guide." It came with you at birth. It's a divine plan for your abundance, purpose, and passion, designed on a soul level just for you.

The thing is, in order to use it, you have to know it's there. Then, you actually have to open it up and read it.

It's like when you purchase a piece of furniture from one of those big box stores. When you get it home, you take all the parts out so you can see what you've got. At first glance, it all makes sense: you can see that these screws go here, and this piece fits with that one. You put it together, thinking you've got it covered, and that you don't *really* need to read that inch-thick instruction manual. You're smart enough to screw together an end table without help, right?

Then, when you're done, you notice that there are a few parts left over. "No big deal," you think. "They're just some spare boards and screws." But then, a few months later, when your table is sagging and wobbly, you realize that it isn't really doing what you intended it to do—which is hold your stuff without falling over.

At that point, do you blame the table, and call it defective? Or do you go back to the instruction manual and figure out the best way to put all the parts together? Maybe that board you ignored was there to stabilize everything. Maybe those extra screws really were necessary.

It's the same with your Wealth Code. Without knowing what your inner instruction manual says, you can be tempted to ignore those parts of yourself that don't immediately fit your picture of how things should be. The difference is that, with an end table, it's easy to see your mistakes and correct them. On the other hand, when things don't seem to be working in your career or your life, it's easy to get disappointed and think that there's something wrong with you, instead of going back to that set of internal directions and reconfiguring your setup and priorities.

Things get even more complicated when you factor in other people. Imagine that, while you're trying to build your end table, you have a crowd of people around you, all shouting out different directions and ideas about what's possible for your new furniture. With that kind of distraction, it would be super easy to put a piece in the wrong place, or forget a screw here and there. The career and life directions you receive from others amount to pretty much the same thing. Sometimes, those directions are valuable; sometimes they're completely off-base. But one thing is always true: if you listen to others' directions without consulting your personal, divine plan for wealth, you're pretty much guaranteed to end up with a wobbly table.

That's what happened to Samantha.

Samantha is a very confident, grounded, and powerful woman who worked in an educational field. She was skilled at running a team, at helping others find their ideal careers, and at managing a lot of different things simultaneously. Whenever her family, friends, or coworkers needed anything, they always came to her—even if they needed a place to live! She was the number-one problem solver in her world.

The thing was, her passion wasn't in education, but in health and wellness. She had a wellness business on the side, and felt that she could really express her purpose there. But after over-giving all day long in every other area of her life, she didn't have the bandwidth to get her business off the ground.

More, she had a problem with receiving. She could give what seemed like an infinite amount of energy to others, but she couldn't ask for it for herself, or receive it fully when it was offered to her. This, combined with a related belief that she couldn't receive what she needed to survive from her wellness business, kept her stuck in a wobbly-table life that didn't feel fulfilling.

What she discovered, as she worked with her Sacred Wealth Code, was that part of her wealth was *receiving*—not just money, but also energy, love, and time. She was stuck in the energy of over-giving, a shadow aspect of her Wealth Code. We cleared the misguided beliefs running behind the scenes that kept her doing things for others in order to feel worthy and loved. Once that energy was gone, it was easy for her to learn to say no to the things that weren't really hers to do, and put all of that extra energy toward the work she knew in her heart was aligned with her purpose. More, by tapping into what she really wanted to give, she opened up to receive what others wanted to share with her, and was able to create a prosperous and thriving business.

A byproduct of aligning with her Wealth Code was that Samantha found and married the love of her life. When you align with what true wealth is for you, everything that fulfills you starts to fall into place!

Another of my clients, Julie, had a foot in two very different worlds. She had a medical career, and she was an artist. When I met her, she really wanted to understand what her purpose was, because she felt like she had a calling beyond what she was doing, but couldn't put her finger on what it was.

She was truly passionate about her art, and had been painting for a long time. She'd even sold a few pieces, but didn't believe that she could make a real living through her art. And so, she waffled back and forth between her career and her passion, without being fully rooted in either.

When we looked at her Sacred Wealth Code, we found that Julie is a teacher and healer, and art is one of her mediums. When she got in touch with that truth inside herself, she discovered that, if she was willing to trust herself and her value, she could teach her art in a way that would help people heal. She was already healing in her medical career, so this was just a new expression of that desire.

After that, she started to sell paintings. She also began to teach, and followed through on an inspiration to create a system designed to bring people together in community and teach them through the act of painting. She even took her new modality to the medical field she'd been involved in.

There were some bumps in the road at first. Julie had historically been very shy about her art, and tried not to let it "interfere" in her medical career. When she first brought her art to her peers in the medical community, they were happy for her, but also reacted as though what she was doing was a hobby. They were willing to let her teach classes, but they didn't want to pay her.

Julie realized that, by not "owning" her art, she was undervaluing one of her greatest gifts, and therefore undervaluing herself. Once she shifted those beliefs and misconceptions, everything changed. Her medical peers and the administration responded by eagerly requesting the work she was bringing to them, and even set up a space in the medical facility where anyone could come and partake in the creative expression and healing she was offering. People came out of the woodwork to purchase her paintings, even though she wasn't advertising them!

Remember, your Sacred Wealth Code resides where your prosperity and purpose meet. For Samantha, it was where her desire to serve met her passion for vitality and health. For Julie, it was at the unlikely intersection of medicine and art. Your "sweet spot" is unique to you. To uncover it, you will need to open up your soul's instruction manual for a wealthy life. When you discover your purpose for wealth, you can lay out all of your component parts—your visions, your passions, your dreams, your talents—align them with your high-value gifts, and begin to see what your Sacred Wealth Code has been waiting to reveal.

As with a high-performance race car, you have no idea what your Sacred Wealth Code can actually do for you until you have cleared the road and can unleash its power under optimal conditions!

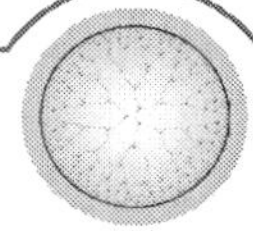

Wealth Focus

Reflection

Journal about or meditate on the following statement:

"If I tell myself the truth ..."

What's one way I am uniquely designed for wealth?

When was the last time I used that unique gift to successfully create wealth?

What stories have I been telling myself about money and success that do not support me in creating the wealth I want?

What is one misconception I have that is holding me back from creating the wealth I want?

Action Steps

Write about what life would be like if you no longer carried your misconceptions about wealth.

Write about what would be possible for you in your life and/or business if you no longer had any misconceptions about wealth.

Identify your "wealth gift" from the reflection section on the previous pages. Over the course of the next twenty-four hours, use that gift to take one practical action in your life or business.

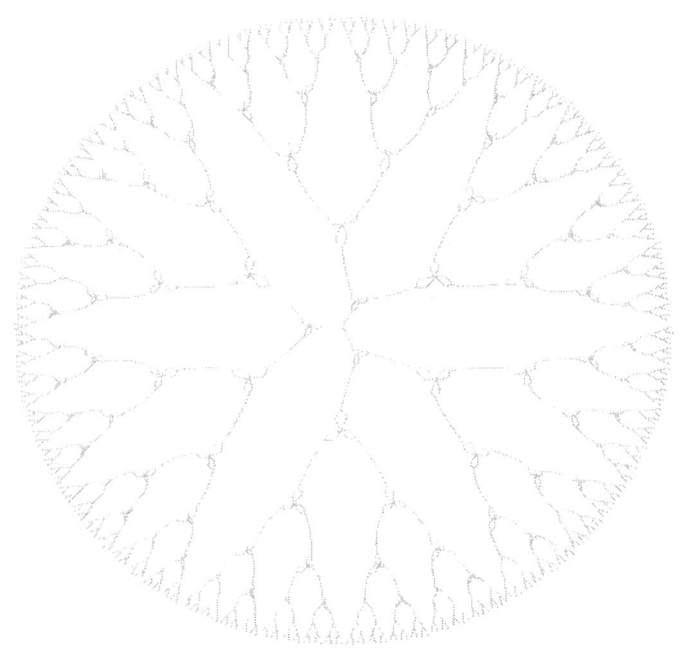

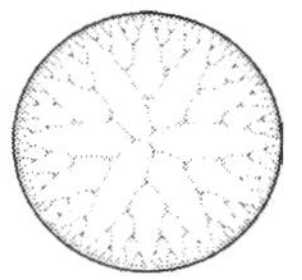

Chapter Three

THE POWER OF YOUR SACRED WEALTH CODE

In the sacred Hindu text, *The Bhagavad Gita*, Sri Krishna says to his disciple, Arjuna, "It is better to strive in one's own *dharma* than to succeed in the *dharma* of another. Nothing is ever lost in following one's own *dharma*. But competition in another's *dharma* breeds fear and insecurity."

In translation, *dharma* equates to purpose, the path that a person walks which is most in alignment with him- or herself and what he or she came here to do. So, the above passage could also be translated, "It's better to live in your own purpose than to succeed in someone else's."

What does this have to do with your Sacred Wealth Code? Everything!

In Indian philosophy (of which Vedic Astrology is a part), there are four primary aims of life, collectively called *puruṣārtha*. These four aims are *dharma* (purpose), *artha* (wealth and acquisition), *kama* (fulfillment of desires), and *moksha* (liberation). In the sequence of attainment, *artha* follows *dharma*. Wealth follows purpose, because wealth is what we need to fulfill our purpose.

This may sound esoteric and "woo-woo," but it's not. Even the esoteric ceases to be lofty when you apply it to real life.

We can only fully access our personal Sacred Wealth Code when we are living in our own purpose, our own *dharma*. However, almost everything we are taught about marketing, wealth acquisition, and success asks us to follow someone else's formula—and therefore, someone else's purpose. Traditional marketing techniques don't work for everyone because not everyone has the Sacred Wealth Code elements that make their purpose compatible with these techniques.

If you're following a path that doesn't align with how you were designed for wealth, you will quickly feel tired, burned out, disillusioned, and frustrated. You might see only a fraction of the success that others who have different Sacred Wealth Codes than you (and therefore different purposes, paths, and internal designs for wealth) have achieved using the same formulas. You might start to feel miserable in your life and work. You might start to hate the business you used to love. You might end up losing your job, your relationships, and even your self-respect because you're wasting so much energy, effort, and soul force trying to fit yourself into a mold that doesn't support who you are, or what you came here to do.

Even if you're not personally at that point, you probably know people who are. Think of someone who has had a business blow up in their face, or has been taken to their knees when their grand plans failed on every front. Or, think of someone who has made a lot of money, but lost everything that was important to them in the pursuit. Chances are, they were following someone else's map to money, not the one encoded in their soul blueprint.

That's why it's so important to understand how *you* are designed, at a soul level, to connect with, attract, and acquire wealth. And it's why I want to teach you to discover and embody this design in every aspect of your life, and use it to consciously create the success to which your soul aspires.

Now, with that in mind, think of the people you know who seem to be *truly* wealthy—not just because of how much money they have, but because they emanate a deep sense of satisfaction. They have a business or career that fulfils them, relationships that support them, and freedom to do what makes them happy. Chances are, their wealth isn't only connected to their money, but to every area of their lives. Did you think that these people were simply lucky, or destined for wealth? Or can you see, now, how they might simply be living in a way that is connected to and aligned with their Sacred Wealth Codes?

Your soul already knows what you should be doing to manifest the wealth that you desire. Your soul already knows what you should be doing to make money. You just need to learn to listen to and follow through on that inner knowing.

FOLLOW YOUR GIFTS, FIND YOUR PURPOSE

Before you start attracting wealth, you need to connect fully to your purpose. But what do you do when you don't have a clue what your purpose *is*?

Your purpose—as written in your Sacred Wealth Code—can be found by tracing the paths of your high-value gifts and talents. These aren't just the things you can do well (chances are there are lots of those), but the things that *no one else can do like you do.*

You see, you're not meant to do everything. None of us are. We all have lots of "secondary" gifts and talents, but these won't always point us toward our purpose. They simply keep us busy.

By the time I turned twenty, I had already worked in two

dozen different jobs. I needed to make money to support myself, so I took whatever job came my way. Sometimes, I worked two or three jobs at the same time. I was a cook, a waitress, and an administrator. I even worked in construction for a while.

None of them lasted very long. I was good at all of them, but I quickly got bored because they didn't have meaning for me. They didn't feed my soul.

You see, what I was really superb at was using my intuition to guide people and teach them how to live in greater alignment. I could make money doing a lot of things, but it wasn't until I poured my heart and soul into my high-value gifts that I started to create *wealth*.

There were a lot of steps along the path to my purpose. Motherhood was one of them. I always knew that I wanted to be a mom and am blessed with two amazing children. In the early years I decided to be a stay-at-home mom for my kids. Even later, when I went back to work full-time, I arranged my schedule around theirs, so I could be available as their parent.

I had been practicing yoga for many years, and teaching here and there, but not formally, and not for money. (Remember, I wasn't valuing my high-value gifts.) Then, one day, my chiropractor told me that he wanted to open a yoga studio, and that he wanted me to teach for him.

"Who, me?" I asked.

At first, I was scared. I ran through so many scenarios in my head. Even though I'd been studying yoga since I was seventeen years old, and had been teaching for a while, I didn't consider myself a *real* teacher, let alone an expert. But after some internal debating, I decided to go for it, and stepped into being paid for my gifts as an intuitive and spiritual teacher for the first time. I could feel in my gut that it was the right thing to do.

A whole new world opened up for me. I was following my Sacred Wealth Code.

Not long after that, I opened my own studio, Yoga and Beyond. I thought I was living in alignment with my high-value gifts and talents, and had created a space that would support that. But because money was tight, I wasn't just teaching and guiding. I was trying to do *everything* in my business—even the daily tasks that tapped into my lower-level skills, like organizing and administration. I had created an opportunity to use my high-value gifts, but I was wearing myself out working on everything else!

You see, we're not meant to do everything. We live in a co-collaborative universe where everyone has a different set of high-level gifts. Our souls thrive in a circle of giving and receiving. When we set aside our high-value gifts in favor of "getting things done" or saving money, we aren't creating wealth. We're pushing it away, because we're avoiding our purpose.

The same thing applies when we follow a career path that doesn't fit our soul blueprint for wealth and fulfillment. So often, we're told as young people that we need to have a certain set of skills, a certain degree, a certain career to be successful and create wealth. But this simply isn't true. As long as we are firmly on the path of our personal purpose and *dharma*, our *artha*—our wealth—will inevitably follow.

My daughter is a perfect example of this. Since she was a very young child, she has been profoundly artistic. She's worked in every medium: drawing, painting, photography, you name it. She bounced from one to the other as she developed her personal style of creation.

Watching her, you could tell that she was soul-guided. She would take the skills she learned in one format and bring them to another. Every new piece of art was a growth process.

As she got older, some confusion set in. She loved her art, but didn't know if she could make a career out of it. Having wealth was very important to her, but she didn't really like academics, and wasn't sure that she wanted to go to college. She struggled with the messages she was receiving from her teachers and peers about the "right" paths to success, and which careers would earn her the money she wanted to make.

Then, the solution appeared. She'd been cutting people's hair since she was twelve. Her friends, her brother's friends, our family—everybody came to her. It was just something fun to do that she was naturally gifted at. But it was also a path that could be turned into a profitable career. After high school, with some nudging from her hairdresser, she decided to go to cosmetology school and get licensed as a hair stylist.

It was like a light was switched on. She became an A student, and rose to the top of her class. "I wish my whole school career had been like this!" she gushed to me one day. "It's so awesome to be doing something I love!"

To my daughter, hair styling isn't just a job: it's her way to create art on the human body. She has a truly amazing gift for bringing someone's inner beauty to the outside, and helping them to shine. More, she can show people how to do this for themselves, every day. She also has the high-value gift of teaching, and now teaches other hair stylists.

Because she stepped into her high-level gifts and talents in such a big way, she also dropped right into that place in her Sacred Wealth Code where purpose and prosperity meet. By the time she was twenty-four, she was making close to six figures, and creating a kind of wealth that was perfectly matched to her soul's desires.

Imagine a world where we are all able to use our greatest gifts and talents in such a way. Seriously, close your eyes and imagine this. Imagine your family, friends, and colleagues devoting their time only to the things they are uniquely good at—the things that enliven them.

Imagine what life would look like, feel like, taste like, if everyone were living in this aligned way. What would your workplace be like? What would your home life be like? What would your friends be talking about? What would you be visioning with them?

This is the promise of purpose.

Use Your Intuition to Find Your Purpose

Your soul already knows what your purpose is, and how you can use it to create wealth through the expression of your Sacred Wealth Code. But do *you* know it, consciously and fully?

"But I'm not intuitive!" you might say. "How can I know what my soul knows?"

Everyone is intuitive. Like our Sacred Wealth Code, intuition is something that we're born with. Some of us have developed our intuition more than others, but just because a skill is dormant doesn't mean it doesn't exist.

You can feel when you're on track with something—when you're enlivened by it, when there's no resistance, and you're willing to dive into it with your whole being. You know when you feel that sense of meaning and movement in your actions. Even if you don't call this intuition, it is.

Your soul is communicating with you all the time, through your feelings, your dreams, and the sensations in your body. Your Sacred Wealth Code is a soul language, and you can feel it speaking in your gut and your heart. You can feel when you're aligned, and you can feel when you're not. All you have to do is pay attention.

I'm sure that you've had one of those experiences where you "just know." You can't *explain* how you know that this is the right action to take, or the right investment to make, or the right job for you to pursue, but you feel that expansiveness, and it can't be ignored.

On the flip side, when you're questioning yourself—when you have that little bit of angst inside, or when your gut is churning—your body is telling you that something is out of alignment. Either you're about to do something that will lead you off-course, or you're operating from a subconscious belief or misconception that's jamming your circuits. With practice, you will learn to tell the difference.

If you're not yet in a place where you can trust the internal voice of your soul to guide you, you're not alone. True soul communication takes practice, but you *can* develop this vital skill.

Here's a simple way to start doing just that.

Hold a piece of fruit or a vegetable in one hand, and then some junk food (like a bag of chips, a candy bar, or something else greasy and sugary) in the other. Notice how the fruit or the vegetable makes you feel when you pay attention to it. Do you feel open? Does your body feel like it's humming with a "yum" or a "yes"? Then, notice how the junk food makes you feel. Chances are (once you get past any sentimental attachment or association around that candy bar or bag of chips), your body will contract and feel heavy.

I rest my case.

Not following your Sacred Wealth Code is like living on junk food. It might taste good at first, but soon you will probably start to feel lost, uncomfortable, or disconnected from yourself. You might be unhappy with the way you look, feel, or function. You don't feel that deep sense of satisfaction when you finish a meal (or a task). You know that if you were making different choices, you would be healthier, wealthier, and more energized, but you don't see a practical way to get there.

Avoiding your Sacred Wealth Code has other consequences, too. You might feel isolated. You might be broke, or you might have a lot of money—but either way, you probably won't be able to hang on to your wealth. You might also be completely shut down emotionally and intuitively, and believe that the idea of being happy and fulfilled by your work is a lie perpetrated by online sales gurus and bright-eyed twenty-somethings with trust funds. You might buy into the lie that the only way to have money is to sell your soul in a job that brings you down instead of lifts you up.

Or maybe all that doom and gloom isn't really where you're at. Maybe life is okay. Just okay, not great ... but not horrible, either. You're not suffering (at least, not on the surface), but you don't have a ton of hope for your future either. Twenty years from now, you'll still be expecting—and receiving—more of the same.

If either of the above sounds like you, it's time to get back on purpose.

Tom spent years climbing the corporate ladder to a well-paying position in the tech industry. It was what he thought he wanted. But because he had his eye on the prize of a big salary, rather than on his high-value gifts and personal purpose, he found himself in a position of being recognized for what the company needed from him, rather than for his actual gifts and talents.

He was good at managing back-end technical systems and support, and was paid well for that skill, but he felt isolated, bored, and burned out. The position and salary he'd worked so hard for lacked meaning for him once he attained them.

Shortly after being promoted, he took a job with another company to try to alleviate his dissatisfaction. In short order he found himself in the exact same situation: well-paid but frustrated, and searching for yet another position with yet another company.

Luckily, Tom discovered his Sacred Wealth Code before he landed that next position. He was a gifted leader with the unique ability to connect with people in a way that brought out the best in them, and inspired them to give their best performance to the job at hand. He also had the gift of "big vision"—being able to see the whole scope of a project, and guide it to completion.

Combined with his practical technical abilities, he was a master at taking a vision and making it a reality.

Because his high-value gifts revolved around leadership and inspiration, working in isolation—as he had at his previous jobs—left him feeling dry and unfulfilled.

Since discovering his Wealth Code, Tom has found a position of vital leadership in a company. His role bridges the gap between front-end sales and back-end technical development. He is on purpose, fulfilled, and thriving in his new job. He also uses his gifts outside of his career to write and produce music—which is another avenue for him to uplift and connect with others.

As you can see, living on purpose doesn't have to mean letting go of everything you're currently doing, or everything you've worked for. It simply means shifting your focus to the place where your highest-level gifts and talents intersect with your dreams for wealth and prosperity. Once you do this, like Tom, you will feel more fulfilled and excited about your work, your life, and your future.

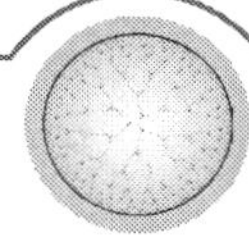

Wealth Focus

Reflection

Journal about or meditate on the following statement:

"If I tell myself the truth ..."

What do I think my purpose is (even in a general sense)?

What is one way I have been following my purpose in my life and work?

Where in my life have I not been following my purpose?

When have I followed my feelings of connection and made an aligned choice because of them? What was the result?

When have I ignored my gut feeling and made a decision that wasn't aligned with my purpose? What was the result?

If I had no need to "work," how would I spend my days? What would I put my energy and drive into?

When I was a young child, what was the dream or career I really wanted to pursue?

How can I use my "wealth gift" (from the previous section) to take one practical action today?

Action Steps

1 Take a moment to celebrate the most positive, aligned choices you have made—even if they happened long ago. Remember how it felt to operate from that place of inner certainty.

2 Write down one thing, situation, or area of life around which you would like to trust your "gut feelings" more.

____

____

____

____

____

Check in with your gut feelings before you make any decisions about that area of your life today.

3 Choose one of the things you identified in the reflection section as something you would put your energy into if you were already wealthy. Then, do that thing today.

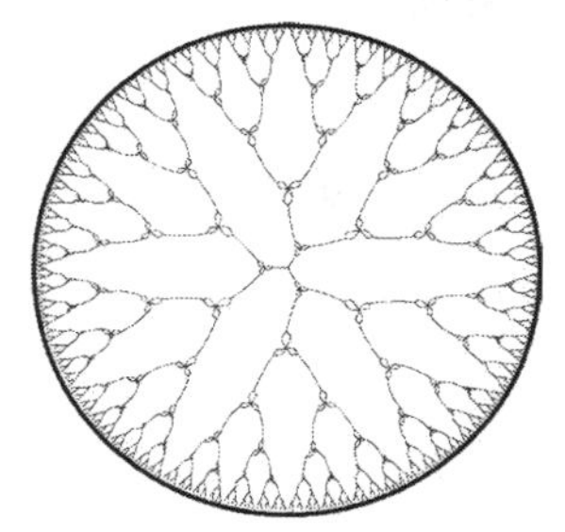

Part II

THE 4 PILLARS OF YOUR SACRED WEALTH CODE

The 4 Pillars

Your Sacred Wealth Code is encoded in your soul at the moment of your birth.

Whenever you engage with anything that speaks to your soul, or connects you with your soul, you have entered the "neighborhood" of your Sacred Wealth Code. From that place of connection, you have access to your soul blueprint and your deepest truths. If you pay attention in those moments, you will be able to *feel* yourself moving into alignment with your Self, your soul, and your Sacred Wealth Code. It may feel a bit like turning onto your safe and familiar home street after a long road trip.

Even if you don't consider yourself naturally intuitive, you will be able to sense when you enter this alignment. It's simply a matter of trusting yourself, your inner knowing, and the sensations in your body.

As you progress through this section and learn the Four Pillars of the Sacred Wealth Code, I want you to take the information I present and apply it in your life in a real, tangible way, every day. Try new things. Think new thoughts. See what feels congruent, light, or "like home," and what doesn't. The more you practice, the more you will be able to tell when you are walking in your soul's neighborhood. The closer you get, the more powerfully you will feel the "rightness" of what you are doing.

The Four Pillars of the Sacred Wealth Code are the four areas which *must* be in alignment for you to find your personal "sweet spot" for wealth. They are like power portals into the heart of your Wealth Code: step into them fully, and you will end up very close to that intersection of purpose and prosperity in your soul's home neighborhood.

THE 4 PILLARS OF YOUR SACRED WEALTH CODE

1. **Purpose**
2. **Prosperity**
3. **Your High-Value Gifts and Talents**
4. **Your Greatest Challenges**

If you did a double-take on that last one, I understand—but you didn't read it wrong. Your greatest challenges *are* part of your Wealth Code, because challenges are almost always the gateways to gifts. The things that really push your buttons are the things that, once resolved, will skyrocket your wealth, success, and fulfillment.

When you fully understand these Four Pillars, and can give them all equal weight in your life, choices, and actions, you will be anchored in your Wealth Code, and the magic will start to happen. Once you've found that "sweet spot," nothing can force you to leave it unless you choose to go.

In each of the chapters in this section, we will explore one pillar of your Wealth Code, and connect to it in a deep, transformative way. Be sure to actively engage with the Wealth Focus exercises, and pay attention to the way you feel as you do so. Get used to navigating by the compass of your intuition, and see where it leads you!

Aligning with your Sacred Wealth Code is like playing a full-contact sport. You can't just *think* your way to it. Connecting with your soul is an experiential process, so I encourage you to get in there and play full-on with the exercises I'll provide in the next several chapters.

Set aside some quiet time to work with and absorb the material in each chapter. Journal about what's revealed to you. Make your own lists in addition to the ones I ask you to create. Do whatever it takes for you to feel connected to your inner truths and fully understand each of the Four Pillars of your Wealth Code.

You may want to work on one chapter per day, or set aside enough time to tackle all four in your own personal "workshop." There is no right or wrong way to do this. Whatever you discover will be right for you. Approach the process like you are getting to know a new friend. Get curious about what this work has to offer. I promise that, each time you revisit it, you will dive a little deeper.

After all, the new friend you are getting to know is you.

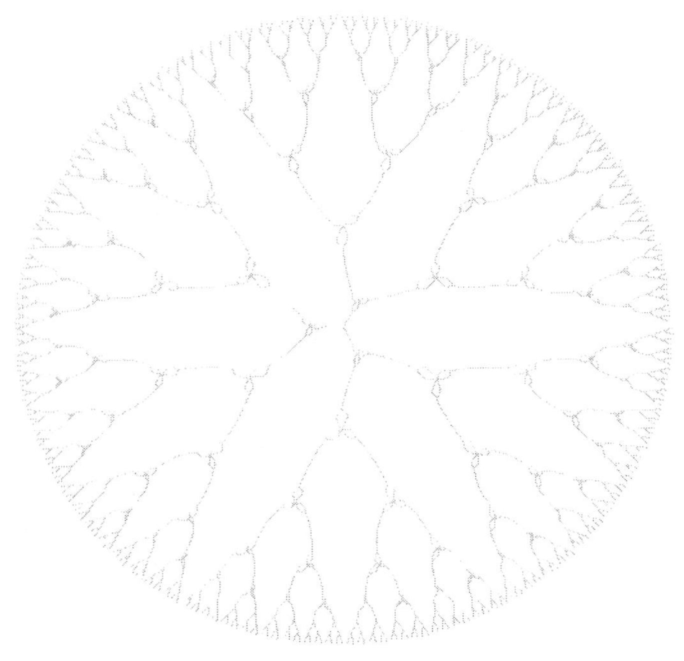

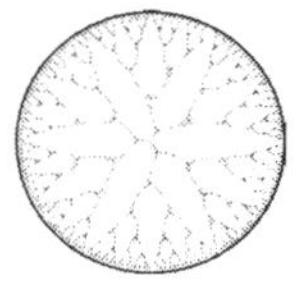

Chapter Four

PILLAR 1: YOUR PURPOSE
HARNESSING YOUR SOUL'S "BIG WHY"

I've discussed the idea of "purpose" several times so far in this book, so chances are you already have a sense of what it means. In this chapter, we'll dive much deeper, and get to the heart of your purpose and how it can help you access and align with your Sacred Wealth Code.

Your purpose is your "big why." It's the driving force behind your thoughts, choices, and actions. It's present whether you recognize it or not—whether you understand it or not. If you are alive, purpose is very, very present in your life.

When you know you want something, you'll take action to get it. But as we all know, not all actions generate results. In order to get in touch with your purpose around this thing, you need to know *why* you want it. (That's why we spent so much time in Chapter One identifying the "why" behind your desire for wealth!)

When you look closely at your own motivations, desires, and inner drivers, you will start to see some commonalities.

Why do you want money, a nice car, a big house? Chances are, it's because you want to feel a certain way in your life. Maybe you want to feel secure and stable. Maybe prestige matters to you. But *why* do you want to feel that way? Why are these things important to your soul? Do you *really* want money—or do you want freedom? Do you *really* want prestige, or do you want to feel valued? Figure that out, and you will find a piece of your Wealth Code and your soul purpose.

THE "WHY" IN YOUR WEALTH VISION

In Chapter One, you told yourself the truth about what the wealth you want really looks like, and what it will make possible for you. You wrote out a vision. Now, we'll revisit that vision and peel back the layers to uncover the purpose behind it.

(If you didn't do the exercises in Chapter One, go back and do them now, before you read any further. Do this as a gift to yourself. Don't hold back, and don't gloss anything over.)

Wealth Alignment Practice 1

Bring out your vision for a life of wealth and abundance. Sit with it. Immerse yourself in it. Close your eyes, take a deep breath, and put your hand on your heart.

See yourself in that wealthy life you desire. Feel that life. Taste it. Smell it. Touch it in your mind. Notice who is with you, and what you're doing. Notice what your priorities are in this wealthy life, and where you're making a difference.

Then, let this question drop into the very center of your heart: "Why do I want this wealthy life—this vision of wealth—above all others?"

Don't search for an answer right now. Just sit

back and watch the ripples of this question spread throughout your being like the ripples in a still pond after you toss in a pebble. Notice what comes up for you. You might hear words, or feel a sensation in your body. You might see a symbol, a color, or a vision. Just absorb it.

Then, after a few minutes have passed, open your eyes, and write down what you experienced.

You need to know the "why" of your vision for wealth because your why is what your soul wants. It's what you're being driven toward, consciously and subconsciously, every day.

If you go into confusion or feel like you're not getting any information from this exercise, it doesn't mean you've failed or done it wrong. Just give yourself a bit more time to sit with your vision. Repeat the exercise in a day or so, and write down everything about your why that comes to you in the meantime.

Don't worry about whether what you're sensing or receiving is the "right" answer. And don't go all altruistic and try to force yourself to align with a "good" purpose. You can serve the world in many ways, not all of which fall into obvious "service" categories.

When it comes to uncovering your Sacred Wealth Code, your purpose isn't what you want to accomplish, or how you want to serve. It's simply the "big why" behind your wealth dream—the force that drives you to seek fulfillment.

As we discussed in Chapter Three, the physical reality of wealth follows purpose. But when you're looking for your purpose, your wealth vision—the *feeling* you want to create through wealth—will point your way.

Here's the cool thing about purpose: it will pull you forward.

When you're in alignment with your "why" for wealth, your purpose will pull you forward—and your tangible, material wealth will follow, because *wealth is everything you need to fulfill your purpose.*

So again, don't get hung up on finding a "good" purpose or the "right" purpose. Whatever answer came through in the exercise on the previous pages is the purpose you will work with for the remainder of your journey through this book.

Trust in this purpose. Even if it doesn't feel "big" enough, it's more than enough to go on. Your soul knows the way. It may just take a while for your conscious brain to catch up!

How to Work With Your "Big Why"

I've already shared that money equals freedom for me. One part of my purpose is to have the freedom to create anything I want, do anything I want, and help anyone I want. I know that wealth and money can give me those opportunities, and so my "big why" for wealth is freedom—and creating freedom for myself and others is my purpose.

So now, knowing a bit more about your own why, I want you to get still and quiet, and ask yourself a second question:

"What is my wealth going to make possible for me?"

For example, your answer might be something like, "To be able to do the work I love, and not have to compromise my joy in order to have what I need and desire."

Feel the power of that vision. Imagine yourself having that, doing that, creating that. Write down whatever images, sensations, and words come up for you.

This process is all about getting to your soul truth around your purpose. So take all the time you need to peel back the layers. What you're doing right now is turning over all the boulders in your mind, and looking at what's living underneath them. As you turn over stone after stone, you will eventually find the roots of the truth you're looking for.

Keep asking the questions in this chapter until you get to the root of your wealth vision, and the true nature of your desire for wealth. If you start getting the same answers over and over, you'll know that you're on to something.

My client Ruby discovered that the root of her wealth vision was freedom, well-being, and security. Having these things would give her the confidence to move away from teaching children, and become the "teachers' teacher" she was actually wired up to be in her Sacred Wealth Code.

With this in mind, Ruby followed her purpose. She left the classroom and started her own business teaching children language according to her own unique teaching philosophies. She then used that business as a springboard to engage other teachers in the work she was doing. She was invited to teach her process at a school, and gathered private clients as well. This new business model not only felt more fulfilling and aligned to her, but it paid well, too!

Celia's purpose for wanting more wealth was the freedom to teach art in her own way, and to create art at her leisure. When I met her, she was working for an organization, as well as doing some private teaching and coaching around art.

As she worked to become more aligned with her Sacred Wealth Code, Celia received a number of great opportunities. One was to work with some prestigious new clients who actually sought her out. Another was to teach at a university.

Continuing to stay true to her purpose, she landed her dream job—a position where she was hired to do what she had originally been doing in her private business. She was paid to create a similar program in a company where she commanded a fantastic salary, and even got to hire her own team.

The result of stepping into her Sacred Wealth Code was different than she'd originally thought it would be. There were so many incredible opportunities coming her way that she was actually thrown off-center. However, by taking the time to sit with each new choice and weigh it against what she understood to be her purpose—freedom, and her desire to support others in their creativity—and her Sacred Wealth Code, she was able to make decisions with confidence, and wholeheartedly accept her dream job without feeling like she had "missed out" or chosen the wrong path.

When it was time to surrender my yoga center, I was in the throes of change, and contending with my own wealth myths and misconceptions. During this time, it was crucial for me to reorient myself to my purpose and wealth vision. If I really wanted freedom, I needed to manifest a business and situation that fully expressed that for me.

I wasted a lot of time looking outside of myself for answers as I tried to save my yoga center. But in reality, everything I needed to know, my soul already knew, because it was written in my Sacred Wealth Code. All I had to do was go within.

What I realized was that I wanted to teach people what I had been forced to learn: that the answers we seek are within us, and that living from the inside out is the only way to create true and lasting wealth, joy, and freedom.

In order to help others reach that place, I had to be squeaky clean with myself about my purpose. I'll be honest: it was painful for me to feel free to do my work in the world. It was painful for me to think about creating the community I wanted to create, and support the leaders and change agents I looked up to.

So really, my purpose wasn't just about freedom for its own sake. It was about helping others to create their freedom. My wealth is all of the resources I need to teach and guide people on a soul level to connect with their Sacred Wealth Code and their deepest purpose. Therefore, my wealth isn't just money: it's my health, my well-being, my creative spirit, and ample time to nourish all three.

It may take some time to uncover your deeper purpose—and that's okay. As long as you keep asking the big questions, and take time every day to connect with yourself and hear the messages of your soul, you will always be moving in the right direction. When your "big why" reveals itself as an even *bigger* "why," the seemingly random guidance you've been receiving all along will suddenly fall into place.

MANIFEST A LIFE ALIGNED WITH YOUR PURPOSE

Now that you know the "big why" of your wealth vision, and what your wealth will help you create, it's time to take action and get things moving.

When you take soul-inspired action, you invite the Divine (or Source, or Spirit, or God) to speed your feet in the right direction. So when your soul prompts you to take an action, don't worry about whether that action is "wrong" or "right." Just go for it.

Why is action so important? Because successful manifestation is the direct result of the alignment of vision, action, and emotion.

You are manifesting all the time. You create your own reality with every choice you make. It doesn't matter if your choices are conscious, subconscious, or unconscious. Everything you think, everything you feel, everything you say, everything you do ... You are constantly creating the reality you are experiencing in your life.

You are creating your wealth, or your lack of it. *You* are creating your freedom, or your lack of it.

It's vitally important to envision what you want. It's your vision that puts you in touch with your "big why"—your purpose. But the real propulsion happens when you add emotion to vision, and then act in accordance with that emotion. Emotion is energy in motion.

You see, you can say one thing and feel something entirely different. You can create a vision of wealth—but if you *feel* poor, your wealth will never fully materialize. Emotion is jet fuel for manifestation. What you feel, most often, is what you create—no matter how much your brain says otherwise.

Feelings and emotions, in this context, aren't wishy-washy or impractical. They're certainly not something to be ashamed of. Feelings serve a purpose—and their purpose is to align you, vibrationally, with what you are creating. How you feel *matters*.

Your mind is an amazing tool. It's thinking all the time. But your mind does not have the power to override your heart, and the feelings you feel will, ultimately, determine your reality no matter what your mind has to say about it.

The good news is, you can use the power of your mind to influence your feelings. You can use your imagination to create feeling states, and use your thoughts to reverse negative feelings and become vibrationally aligned with your purpose, wealth vision, and Sacred Wealth Code.

When you are vibrationally attuned to everything you want and desire, those desires will be fulfilled, in one way or another. When your feelings are vibrationally attuned to what you don't want and don't desire, you'll get more of those "don'ts."

You can feel when you're in alignment with your soul, and you can feel when you're not. You can feel when you're aligned with your Sacred Wealth Code, and when you're not. And when you're not sure what direction your soul and your Wealth Code are leading you in, you can use this power of feeling to walk the path in the dark, and trust that your soul will lead you through.

When your feelings are aligned, every action you take will come from a place of soul connection and inspiration. Your actions have consequences—and when your actions support your purpose and your wealth vision, their consequences will be positive, exciting, and even miraculous. If your actions are coming from a place of misalignment, on the other hand, their consequences will push you even further away from your purpose and wealth vision—until you stop, reassess, and course-correct.

Here's an exercise that will help you connect with, and discover how to take, inspired action.

Wealth Alignment Practice 2

Close your eyes, put your hand on your heart, and take a deep breath right into your heart space. Send your gaze and your attention inward. (The simple act of closing your eyes tunes out at least 80 percent of the stimuli around you. Remember, this is an inside-out process!)

Take more deep breaths into your heart, and invite your mind down into your heart. Imagine that there is a slide or a staircase leading from your head to your heart. Invite your mind to make the journey downward, sliding or stepping down through your nasal cavity, your throat, the top of your chest, down into the very center of your heart.

By doing this, you are bringing your mind and your heart together to tap into and understand your soul truth. This is a beautiful marriage. You want to use your mind—but you want your mind to follow the deep wisdom of your heart. So, unify them. Breathe them together. Even if you're not sure this is actually happening, trust that it is.

Now, let the following question drop into your heart, just like you did in the last exercise:

"What is one inspired action I can take today that will support me in becoming aligned with my purpose?"

Sit with whatever comes up. Then, when you feel ready, open your eyes and write it down. No matter how insignificant—or how momentous—it may seem, your soul has just given you a quest to fulfill.

Whatever the action that you were given, take it today. Don't wait. If for some reason you really can't make it happen today (or do it all in one day) open up your calendar and put it on your schedule. If you want to align with your purpose through inspired action, procrastination is your worst enemy, because it tells your mind (and your emotions) that your soul's requests aren't important enough to honor. Don't let yourself get sidetracked. Block off time to take this action. Set a reminder alarm so you don't forget. Do whatever you need to do to make it happen.

Repeat this exercise every time you need to realign yourself with your purpose. Regular check-ins with your soul will keep you vibrationally aligned with your purpose and your wealth vision, and keep your busy mind from wandering away from your soul's path. By taking soul-inspired action, you are consciously collaborating with the Divine (or Source, or Spirit, or God) and developing a deeper level of trust in yourself and the universe. It takes time and practice, but it's worth it. You're worth it!

The three components of successful manifestation are vision, action, and emotion. Your "big why" is your purpose for your wealth vision. Your purpose drives your choices and actions toward your wealth vision. Your feelings and emotions are the vibrational energies that let you know if your choices and actions are in alignment with your purpose and your wealth vision.

When you are "on purpose," you are aligned with your Sacred Wealth Code.

Taking soul-inspired action moves you in the direction you want to go. It's like wind in your sails, and it's blowing in the precise direction of your true wealth.

Your soul has all the answers. It knows what actions to take. By tuning into your heart, and melding your heart and mind, you can access your soul and learn to understand your unique soul language. Anyone can learn to do this—even if it doesn't seem to come naturally.

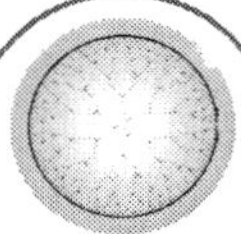

Wealth Focus

Reflection

Journal about or meditate on the following statement:

"If I tell myself the truth …"

What is my purpose for wealth?

____

____

____

____

When I am living in alignment with that purpose, what will be possible for me?

____

____

____

____

What choices have I been making that are aligned with my purpose and wealth vision?

What choices have I been making that are *not* aligned with my purpose and wealth vision?

Do the feelings I feel every day align with my purpose and wealth vision? Why or why not?

Do the actions I take every day align with my purpose and wealth vision? Why or why not?

When was the last time I took inspired action that aligned with my purpose?

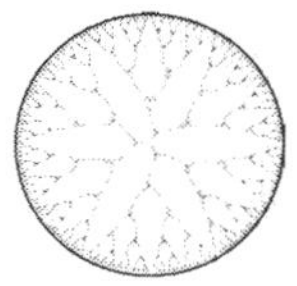

Chapter Five

PILLAR 2: YOUR PASSION THE ESSENCE OF FULFILLMENT

Once you have identified your purpose and the "big why" for your wealth, you are poised to create what you desire.

But working from purpose alone is like sitting in the car with the engine off. You know where you're headed, and why—but you're not moving yet.

That's where *passion* comes in.

Passion is the second pillar of your Sacred Wealth Code, and it's the fuel for your purpose—the horsepower, if you will. It comes from your soul, and it never runs out. When your passion is ignited, you're on the highway to wealth—the kind of wealth that's right and true for you.

Passion is what gets your motor running. It's your portal to pleasure, joy, and fulfillment—to the natural soul state of your being. It's that thing you would do every day if you could—the thing that, no matter how often you do it, never feels like drudgery. It could be anything: baking, reading, dancing, skydiving, mountain climbing, writing, painting, or playing with kids. The activity isn't nearly as important as *the state of being you achieve while engaged in it.*

There's been a lot of research done around the subject of passion, so I won't rehash it all here. However, I will say that without that fuel of passion, you will never fully reach the soul-inspired sweet spot of your Sacred Wealth Code. In fact, you might drive right by the exit ramp, and never know it. You'll keep on going, worn down, burned out, and fed up, until you can't push anymore. You might stay financially broke, or you might just feel spiritually broke. No matter what you accomplish on the outside, living without a direct soul connection to passion won't make your wealth dream come true.

THE PASSION PITCH

When you feel passion in your daily life, you are connected to your soul's natural state of being. Learning to center yourself in your passion is a bit like trying to play a perfectly attenuated note on a violin. There are lots of tones you can play on a violin string, but when you're in the right spot, and perfectly in tune, you can feel the resonance of that note from the top of your head to the tips of your toes.

Now, imagine that your passion is only one string of four on that soul violin. Another is purpose. Your gifts and challenges—the third and fourth pillars of your Sacred Wealth Code—are the final two. If you can learn to play in tune on all of those strings, there will be no song you cannot master.

There is no mistaking resonance. It's either there, or it's not. You can access it in different ways, but you can't fake it.

You become resonant with your passion by doing what you love, in some shape or form. When this is directly connected to your business, your career, your investments, or whatever else you are doing to create wealth, you have access to your Sacred Wealth Code—and, better yet, your Sacred Wealth Code has access to you.

Your wealth hangs out with your passion. If the Four Pillars of your Wealth Code are the strings of your soul violin, your Sacred Wealth Code is the body. Neither is complete without the other. So, if you're playing in resonance with your purpose and passion, your Sacred Wealth Code is humming along.

The more you ignite your passion on a daily basis, the more access you will gain to your Sacred Wealth Code, and the easier it will be for you to sink into that resonant state of being. This doesn't always have to take place around your work. You can drop into your passion by doing what you love, hanging out with people who inspire you, having thoughtful conversations, moving your body, walking in nature, or making art. You can even get in touch with your passion by watching other people engage with their own passions—like by watching a play or dance performance, visiting an artist's studio, or relaxing with a great book.

Personally, I know that I can always pluck my passion string through hiking, connecting deeply with the people I love, and listening to music. When I engage in any of these activities, I feel soul-connected and resonant for hours afterward.

How about you? What are you passionate about?

If you're not sure, this exercise is an easy way to find out.

Wealth Alignment Practice 3

Grab a paper and pen, sit down, and close your eyes. Take a deep breath. Let your mind begin its journey down into your heart. Let them meet, and meld.

Once you feel calm and aligned, let this question drop into your heart: "What ignites my passion?"

Take another deep breath, and then write down anything and everything that comes to mind.

Now, ask yourself, "What have I done in the last seven days to access my passion? How about in the last month? The last year?"

Write down every instance you can think of where you engaged in an activity related to your passion.

Finally, ask, "What do I wish I could do every day to stay resonant with my passion?"

Write for at least one minute. Write down everything that comes up for you. Don't censor yourself. Just let it all pour out. Remember, there is no "wrong" way to access your passion. It's not about the activity itself: it's about the resonance you feel when you're engaged in that activity.

When you're ready, we'll take it a step further.

Look at what you've written. Is there some common thread that bonds all your passion activities? Maybe they all involve being in nature. Maybe they're all related to reading and words. Maybe they're centered around food, or movement, or sensation. Pick up those common threads and hold them in your mind. Those threads are your passion—the fuel that will propel you into your Sacred Wealth Code, and give you the momentum to operate from that resonant place.

When your actions to manifest wealth are lit up by your passion, you will create your wealth dream faster and more easily than you could if you were relying on purpose alone. Remember, purpose pulls you forward—but passion is fuel.

When you regularly spend time in resonance with your passion, doing things that you are passionate about and that feel inspiring, you are ten, twenty, even a hundred steps closer to creating prosperity. **When you know how to drop into that passion space, and play that resonant note, your passion will reveal itself in your career, your business, and your service to the world.**

Being engaged with your passion on a daily basis takes practice. It's not always easy. There are a hundred tasks that we all have to accomplish every day, and most of them will probably feel like they extinguish your passion rather than ignite it. Where you put your attention is key to keeping that fire burning. Even if you own your own business, you need to know where to spend that precious currency of passion and attention so that your Wealth Code can work through you, and you don't get distracted or burned out. (Remember, no one is meant to do everything!)

Liz was a successful voiceover artist and actress with a lucrative media career. But as she grew older and changed soul cycles, she lost her passion for what she was doing. (In Vedic Astrology, your soul goes through several planetary cycles during your lifetime, each of which last for a number of years. During the transition from one cycle to another, your soul will nudge you to develop certain personal qualities, and develop or expand particular areas of your life.) During her soul cycle shift, Liz thought that the part of her life which revolved around media was over, but she wasn't sure how she wanted to manifest wealth next, or what her work in the world would be.

She loved hiking and mountaineering, and started spending more time in those pursuits. Being in nature fired her passion and made her feel more connected—not just to her soul, but to the entire world. She toyed with the idea of creating a business that would bring teens and young adults in touch with nature, but it wasn't quite the right fit.

As she spent more time in resonance with her passion, and contemplated her wealth dream and purpose, Liz realized that her work path didn't lead into the mountains—at least, not directly.

The mountains were there to nourish and rejuvenate her, but they weren't the nexus of her Sacred Wealth Code.

As she followed her inner guidance, stayed resonant with her passion, and took inspired action regularly, her new path was revealed—and it led straight to the junction of her passion, purpose, and wealth dream. Soon, she was being invited to do voiceover work for programs that aimed to bring awareness to preserving our precious natural environment. Her passion for the mountains would be channeled through her high-level gifts—voiceover work and acting—to serve her purpose and create the wealth she needed to continue that service in a passionate, fully-fueled way.

When these new opportunities manifested, Liz was thrilled. Her Sacred Wealth Code had spoken through her, and shown her the way to create exactly what she desired. She was making a difference in a big way, and using her unique gifts to uplift the world while attracting wealth and feeding her passion.

It took time for Liz to fully realize the nature of her new path, but she was able to stay on track by tuning in regularly to her wealth dream, her purpose, and her passion. She followed her inner signals step by step, like following the instructions from her inner satellite GPS, and eventually, that guidance led her straight to her Sacred Wealth Code.

Your Sacred Wealth Code is communicated to you through the voice of your soul, and the voice of your soul can only be heard when you are completely attuned to your own natural resonance—aka, your passion. Taking the time to regularly feed your passion—even when it isn't obviously connected to your work path—isn't selfish or wasteful. It's absolutely necessary if you want your Sacred Wealth Code to reveal itself in your life.

WHERE PASSION MEETS WEALTH

There are things that you're passionate about—and then, there are things that you're passionate about around creating wealth.

Whether you're currently doing them or not, there are things in the world of business or career that light you up, and things that don't. Maybe you love sales and marketing, or generating new ideas. Maybe it lights you up to execute those ideas, lead a team in completing a project, or bring others' ideas to life with creativity and color. Maybe you love managing the details of an administration, or maybe you'd prefer to be the person in charge of the company who makes the big decisions.

We're going to take a few moments right now, and delve into your passions around wealth creation.

Wealth Alignment Practice 4

Gather up your pen and paper, get into your still space, and guide your brain down to meet with your heart.

Take several deep breaths, and then ask yourself, "What am I passionate about in terms of manifesting wealth?"

Take another deep breath, and then write for one to three minutes about whatever comes up for you. Just like last time, don't censor yourself. You want to keep an open channel from your soul to your paper.

Once you've run out of things to write, read your list. Circle the top three items that really stand out for you.

Then, look back at the list of passions you created in the last section, and circle the top three things on that list that stand out for you.

(This doesn't mean that you're discounting the other items on your lists, just that you're targeting your energy right now. We're looking for the most concentrated level of your passion.)

Now, compare the two. How do your top "wealth creation" passions intersect with your "I'd do this every day" passions? Can you think of anything that would allow you to access both at the same time?

Ask yourself, "What's one inspired action I can take today to be in resonance with my passion?" Write down the answer you receive.

Next, ask yourself, "What is one inspired action I can take today to be in my passion around wealth?" Write that answer down, too.

Then, take both of those actions within the next twenty-four hours.

Now, take out your calendar and schedule at least one activity from your "I'd do this every day" list and one activity from your "wealth creation passions" list per day for the next month (or more). Your aim is to build your passion into your life so that you can be in the neighborhood of your Sacred Wealth Code regularly. Soon, you'll be directly connected to your Wealth Code, and opportunities will start to flow to you—the same way they did for Liz in the story from the previous section!

Here's another great example of "I'd do this every day" passion and "wealth creation passion" linking up to create a new life path for someone.

Maggie is a fantastic marketer. She has a business archetype in her Sacred Wealth Code, along with a creative Visionary aspect, so she's quite a powerhouse as an entrepreneur. However, she wasn't feeling much passion around her marketing business. She had tried different online business models and other avenues, but she wasn't having the success she wanted. Despite the time, money, and energy she was investing into her business, it just wasn't working out.

Understandably, she was getting frustrated. She didn't understand how, with all her business talents, she couldn't make what she was doing work. In her mind, she knew it *should* work, and that online business was where her wealth was. But something was in the way.

When she and I met, I knew right away where the issue lay. Maggie was missing the passion piece. Her passion wasn't in the nuts and bolts of business, but in spirituality! She totally geeked out on spirituality, personal development, and anything metaphysical. Her research and practice in that area fed her soul, because spiritual connection is another part of her Wealth Code. She just didn't believe that there was any money in it.

When she realized that she was ignoring a huge part of her passion—and of her Sacred Wealth Code—Maggie did an immediate turnaround. She made a commitment to bringing her passion for spirituality into her work.

The very next day, she landed a $10,000 client.

There is a way to connect your passion with your purpose and the work that you do in the world. It might not be obvious at first, but if you leave your passion out, you'll almost always find yourself struggling—as Maggie did—to figure out what's missing, and why things just never seem to line up.

Your soul is speaking to you. Your passion string is waiting to be played. It's time for you to get in tune.

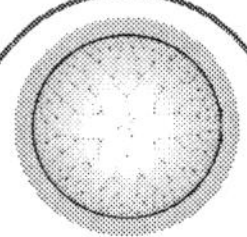

Wealth Focus

Reflection

Journal about or meditate on the following statement:

"If I tell myself the truth ..."

What am I really passionate about doing and feeling in my life?

Am I allowing myself to engage with my passion on a regular basis? Why or why not?

How do I feel about the passions I uncovered in the exercises in this chapter? Am I judging them? Do I think they're silly, or not a "good" use of my time? How can I change that viewpoint?

____

____

____

____

____

____

What happened the last time I fully engaged with one of my passions? How did I feel?

____

____

____

____

____

____

Action Step

Repeat the exercises you encountered earlier in this chapter. In particular, work with the question, “What is one inspired action I can take today?” on a daily basis.

Inspired Actions:

1 ____________________

2 ____________________

3 ____________________

4 ____________________

5 ____________________

6 ____________________

7 ____________________

8 ____________________

9 ____________________

10 ____________________

Be sure to follow through on the instructions you receive!

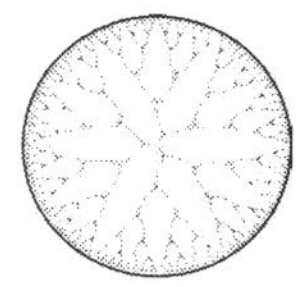

Chapter Six

PILLAR 3: YOUR HIGH-VALUE GIFTS WIELDING YOUR SUPERPOWERS

At the junction of your purpose and prosperity is your Sacred Wealth Code.

If that intersection is your Sacred Wealth Code, purpose and prosperity are the streets that lead there. Passion is the fuel that gets you to that place. And your high-value gifts are the houses that stand at the corners of that intersection.

When you live in, and operate from, your high-value gifts, you are literally positioning yourself in a "house" that overlooks the intersection of your passion and prosperity. You've set up shop in the neighborhood of your soul, the nexus of your own greatness—and so everything you do with your gifts is empowered by your Sacred Wealth Code.

When you don't use your high-value gifts, it's like buying real estate on a different corner. You may be near the road of your passion, or the road of prosperity, but you're not in your soul's neighborhood. You don't have that perfect view of the intersection of purpose and prosperity, or unlimited, full-time access to your Sacred Wealth Code.

Luckily, you have the fuel of your passion. You can use that fuel to explore—to drive around, metaphorically speaking—until you find your Sacred Wealth Code.

DISCOVER YOUR PERSONAL SUPERPOWERS

Most people, in my experience, don't know or understand their high-value gifts. Or, they undervalue them, because they don't seem as bright and shiny (at first glance) as other gifts on their personal roster. But until you find, and implement, your high-value gifts, you'll always feel like you're cruising around the wrong neighborhoods, looking for your home.

Your high-value gifts are yours and yours alone. There are some things that only you can do in the way that you do them. That's why there can be lots of people who have similar businesses and business skills, but all succeed in different ways.

No two people are exactly the same. But sometimes, our conditioning tricks us into thinking that we have to do things like others do them. This belief that we have to follow another's path to succeed is one of the things that keeps wealth at bay. Previously-driven roads will only lead us to that soul-powered intersection if they are perfectly aligned with our Sacred Wealth Code. Otherwise, we will all have to turn off the highway at some point, and make our own way.

Your high-value gifts and talents are your superpowers—and sometimes your superpowers are different, and more subtle, than what you're "good at."

Your superpowers are the things you do that *only* you can do. The way you communicate, the way you inspire others to take action, the way you organize piles of raw data into something comprehensible to others . . . these are high-value gifts and talents.

They aren't necessarily the work you're doing in the world—but they *inform* the work you're doing in the world, and the more time you spend using them, the more you will develop them. When you're using your superpowers to their fullest capacity, your Sacred Wealth Code is working through you to create prosperity.

The following is an example of how high-value gifts and talents work:

A young child has a high-value gift for problem-solving. This helps her excel in mathematics and computer programming—but it also helps her play an instrument, carve things out of wood, and sell her projects on the internet.

As she grows up, she finds new opportunities to use her talent for problem-solving. Her talent expands, and also becomes more precise. She begins to master this superpower, and attract new opportunities to put this power to work—like job offers in STEM fields, or freelance gigs designing web sites.

As long as this young person is given the freedom to choose the opportunities which align not only with her superpower of problem-solving, but also with her passions, dreams, and purpose, she will stay connected to her Sacred Wealth Code. However, too often, she will be directed by well-meaning parents, teachers, and other adults to take a wrong turn, and navigate away from her soul neighborhood.

People who use their high-value gifts from childhood have an incredible level of mastery. Chances are, they are virtuosos in their fields (even if they've changed fields over time), because the work they are attracted to, and ultimately choose, engages their high-value gifts in some form or another. These precious souls are also few and far between. Many more people no longer use the superpowers they possessed in childhood. Instead, they've learned to focus on the lesser gifts and talents that others insisted were more valuable and kept them closer to "the norm."

Many times, our "suppressed" superpowers are talents like intuition, empathy, creativity, or curiosity—talents that aren't obviously valuable in the marketplace, which make people uncomfortable, or which don't fit stereotypical gender roles.

I mean, how many times were you told as a child to "stop asking questions"? How many times did you hear, "Boys/girls/good kids don't do that"? Probably more than you can count!

When I was eleven, I had a dream of playing the trombone. My mom said it was not "ladylike," and that I had to play the violin. (Guess how long *that* lasted? Mere months.)

If you have a gift that's been dormant for a long time, don't worry. You have the freedom to resurrect it. And if you have a gift that you've been using for your entire life, but in an "under the radar" kind of way, you can bring it to the forefront again anytime you want, and start using it to anchor your passion and purpose!

Wealth Alignment Practice 5

Close your eyes, and travel back along the road of your life. Remember the superpowers you possessed as a child. Do you still use those gifts? What opportunities have they brought you? What prosperity have they brought you? What wealth have they brought you? (Note that this wealth may not be only money, but also experiences, gifts, relationships, or anything else that you value.)

Now, ask yourself, "How can I use these gifts more often in my life right now?"

YOU ARE A "SOUL ARTIST"

Your high-value gifts are encoded in your Sacred Wealth Code. When you're using them, you are accessing the currency of prosperity. Your Sacred Wealth Code works through your superpowers—and the actions you take that employ them—to manifest the wealth you need to fulfill your purpose and passion.

Again, there are a lot of misconceptions and cultural programs around wealth and how we create it. Because of these, many people aren't using their high-value gifts. Instead, they're focused on what's needed or wanted in the marketplace. Maybe they received recognition and rewards for using their less-valuable gifts, and started to confuse the things that they're good at with their real superpowers. Or, maybe they were told from a young age, "You can't make money doing that," and steered their paths away from their superpowers to follow a more mainstream career trajectory.

There's a big difference between the things you're good at and your high-value gifts. Chances are, you're good at a lot of things. You have skills that you've developed over your lifetime, and skills that come naturally. But these skills are not your superpowers. You weren't born with them. They don't come from your soul blueprint.

One of the big mistakes I made in my yoga business was not focusing solely on my high-value gifts. I was using some of them—like my ability to teach and intuit, and put together practical systems from spiritual principles that people could use to live from their souls—but I wasn't making them my highest priority. Too much of my energy was focused on administrating and facilitating. I was good at those things, too, but they were skills, not superpowers. They didn't replenish my energy; they drained it. They also pushed me into the shadow side of my Wealth Code. (More on that later.)

Your high-value gifts are like a painter's art, or a musician's unique sound. They express themselves through you in a totally individual way. Every painter has a unique way of putting paint on canvas, and every guitarist has a signature sound and style. It's why you can tell a Da Vinci from a Monet at a glance, and Jimi Hendrix from Robert Plant or Jeff Beck in the space of a few measures. No one else can employ your superpowers the way you can. Your uniqueness is part of the principle of universal expansion.

The search for our superpowers is where we run into our fear of the unknown. We need to follow a road that's off the GPS grid—a road that no one has driven before. It's tempting to keep doing what we're merely good at, what's acceptable—what will help us to fit in.

At a tribal level, we need that sense of belonging. In ancient times, artists, innovators, and thought leaders quickly became outcasts and heretics. The fear of that casting-out remains imprinted on our society to this day, but it's no longer valid. We no longer need to stick with the herd to survive. We can express ourselves as the unique beings we are, and be appreciated for what makes us different rather than what makes us the same. Instead of being outcasts, we can create a new caste—a new category into which we fit perfectly.

Starting right now, regardless of what your superpower is, I want you to think of yourself as an artist—a soul artist—and your high-value gifts as your artistic medium. When you create your art, whatever form it takes, you are expressing the deepest energies of your soul, which is part of the Divine. When you use your superpowers, you are literally acting as the paintbrush of the Divine, coloring our amazing, expanding universe in a bold new way.

I know, that's pretty lofty. So let's bring it down to Earth, and anchor all of this in a way you can actually act on.

There's something called the "5 Percent Rule" that many successful entrepreneurs use. They focus their attention, time, and energy on the 5 percent of their businesses that *only they* can do. That way, they're constantly engaged with their high-value gifts and talents.

Then, they build a community of people whose superpowers complement their own and address the other 95 percent of their businesses. Ideally, everyone in this network is using not only their skills, but their own high-value gifts. Everyone feels happy and fulfilled, and the collective thrives.

Imagine what the world would be like if everyone was using their personal superpowers. Imagine a world, a workplace, a family, a relationship where everyone focused on using their high-value gifts to add value to the collective. Everyone would be on their personal leading edge, learning and growing in a way unique to them, and gifting others with their talents in a totally natural way.

It can happen. But only if you're willing to step into that unknown place, use the fuel of your passion to forge a new path, and find a new home at the intersection of your purpose and prosperity.

Sarah founded a visionary company that designed and manufactured eco-friendly clothes. The company was getting off the ground, but slowly: she needed more investors to take it to the next level. She was also still working her corporate job to pay her bills.

When we started working with her Sacred Wealth Code, Sarah discovered that one of her superpowers was the ability to inspire others through speaking. She could literally magnetize people to her movement just by sharing her story.

Once she knew this, she stopped asking other people to negotiate with possible investors, and started getting on the phone herself. She would speak to these investors about her passion for eco-friendly style, and her mission to change the fashion world.

Within thirty days, she found an investor willing to contribute $40,000—exactly the amount she needed to finish building her first factory and start producing her clothing line.

Access Your Superpowers and Change Your World

It's time to tune in once again, and learn the truths that your soul already knows.

Wealth Alignment Practice 6

Close your eyes, place your hand over your heart, and take a deep breath. Invite your mind and heart to come together. Let your mind slide right down into the center of your chest and connect with the wisdom of your heart and soul.

Let the following questions drop into the stillness of your heart, and watch where the ripples lead.

"What do I do in my own fabulous way, that's natural for me, and that I love to do?"

"If money were not an issue, what would I naturally do, all day long?"

"What do people compliment me for? Why do people seek me out?" (Note: this may not be something you're charging people for.)

"What do I 'geek out' about so much that I want to know everything about it?"

Now, write down everything that came up for you through those questions. Don't censor yourself, or judge what comes through. Just make a list. Write for at least three minutes without pausing.

You now have a list of your greatest gifts and talents!

Now, rate each item on your list from 1 to 5, with 1 being your most unique gifts and talents. Then, circle the five highest-scoring items on your list. (If you have more than five things that you rated with a 1, circle all of them.)

For each of these items, drop in with the following question: "What is one inspired action I can take right now to use this high-value gift to create prosperity?"

Write down every inspired action that comes to you. Then, put each action on your calendar, and do it, without question, even if it doesn't immediately make sense to you.

Some inspired actions that might pop up for you:

- Make a phone call to someone you haven't talked to in a while
- Pay a visit to a certain store, place, or event
- Go for a walk
- Read a certain book
- Listen to a certain album or podcast
- Reach out to a potential client you thought was a "no"
- Revisit a project or design you'd put aside

Whatever comes to you during the exercise on the previous page, it is important that you take those steps. Remember, this is an opportunity to let your Wealth Code blossom, and let the Divine kick your feet in the right direction.

You could also work with your list of high-value gifts in a different way. Take a few moments to identify how you are already using those gifts in the work you're doing right now. Then, think of some ways in which you can bring those gifts into even greater prominence.

Remember: Your high-value gifts are your superpowers. The more that you use them, the more they will grow—and the more they will grow *you*, your opportunities, and your prosperity.

As you bring your superpowers into your daily life, you will discover new ways to use them. Like Sarah in the story from the previous section, you'll be amazed at the doors your gifts open for you.

I started using my high-value gift of turning spiritual truth into practical guidance even before I discovered yoga and Vedic Astrology. My intuitive interest led me to those practices, which in turn led me to open my yoga center. I spent years growing my superpowers, but it wasn't until my center closed that I was able to stop distracting myself with the tasks I was merely good at, and dive full-on into my high-value gifts. This deep dive led me to the body of work I'm doing now—including the revelation of the Sacred Wealth Code and its potential to help others step *directly* into the kind of internal alignment it had taken me so many years to find.

My unique work as a soul artist—my gift to the universe—is the knowledge I've gained along my journey, and my ability to help others unlock their soul blueprints and live directly from their Sacred Wealth Codes. It is because of my life expertise that I am able to use my superpowers in this particular way.

So if you've spent years avoiding, or ignoring, or suppressing your high-level gifts in favor of your more mainstream skills, don't worry. You haven't wasted your time. You've simply gained new avenues through which you can express your Sacred Wealth Code and your personal superpowers.

No life experience is wasted. Everything you've learned has simply been leading you here: to your soul's home at the intersection of your purpose and prosperity.

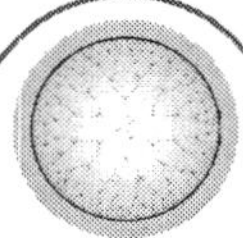

Wealth Focus

Reflection

Journal about or meditate on the following statement:

"If I tell myself the truth ..."

What superpowers have been with me since birth?

What did I love to do, be, and create as a child? Do I still do those things?

How do I feel about the superpowers I uncovered in the exercises in this chapter? Am I judging them? How can I embrace them fully to bring them forward in my daily life?

When was the last time I remember using one of my superpowers?

What happened the last time I fully used one of my superpowers?

Action Step

Repeat the exercises you encountered earlier in this chapter. In particular, work with the question, "What is one way I can use my highest-level gifts?" on a daily basis. Write your daily actions below.

Inspired Actions:

1 ______________________________

2 ______________________________

3 ______________________________

4 ______________________________

5 ______________________________

6 ______________________________

7 ______________________________

8 ______________________________

9 ______________________________

10 ______________________________

Be sure to follow through on the instructions you receive!

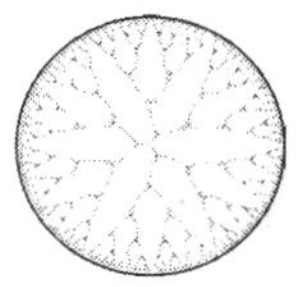

Chapter Seven

PILLAR 4: YOUR GREATEST CHALLENGES THE UNEXPECTED GATEWAY TO WEALTH

You have superpowers.

And, like all superheroes, you also have challenges.

When you start accessing your high-value gifts, it may feel like your challenges are blocking you from fully engaging with your gifts. Or, maybe your gifts are flowing beautifully, but every time you use them, your challenges show up simultaneously, like your gifts' annoying evil twins.

Your challenges are not bad. They're not evil, and they're not part of some cosmic plot to stop you from achieving your wealth dreams and fulfilling your purpose. They are part of your journey, and they are designed to help you grow stronger, dig in deeper, and connect with what you truly believe.

Some of your challenges are soul choices. Whether you know it or not, you have chosen to engage with these obstacles in order to grow within yourself, and learn what you need to know to follow the path of your purpose and live in alignment with your Sacred Wealth Code. The challenges we choose on a soul level are *healthy* challenges. It's like you're a tree, and your challenges are the pruning shears that trim your unnecessary branches. It may be hard at first to feel so bare and exposed, but eventually you will grow taller and stronger because of this pruning.

There are also challenges we force on ourselves because we have decided not to listen to our soul's voice. They're the wrong turns we keep following out of confusion, obligation, stubbornness, or just plain habit. They're the jobs we stay in too long, the relationships we hang on to even when they harm us, the patterns and programming around money and wealth that we know are damaging, but that feel too hard or painful to change. Whatever their origins, however, our self-created challenges are nearly always the results of trying to run away (consciously or subconsciously) from our soul challenges.

Then, finally, there are your unexplainable challenges. The challenges that no one should ever have to deal with. The challenges you wouldn't wish on your worst enemy. I don't know why these challenges happen, but I do know that, if you can get through to the other side, you will claim gifts along the way, and move closer to your soul's neighborhood and your personal superpowers.

As Bruce Lee memorably stated, "Using no way as a way, having no limitation as limitation."

Or, as Mary O'Mally wrote in her book of the same title, "What's in the way *is* the way."

THE SHADOW SIDE OF YOUR SACRED WEALTH CODE

In order to get past your biggest challenges, you have to use your greatest gifts. Your challenges are the hidden, overgrown pathways to your Sacred Wealth Code and the intersection of purpose and prosperity where your high-value gifts live. Your challenges are the grains of sand that shape the pearl, the stones in your shoes that force you to stop running and look around. They are irritating, triggering, and sometimes downright painful. But they are part of your Sacred Wealth Code and your soul blueprint, and although you can avoid them, you can't make them go away until you confront them fully, and grow in the ways they require.

If you've been avoiding your superpower gifts, chances are that you have also, to some degree, been avoiding your challenges. However, until you apply your gifts to them, these challenges will keep appearing in different ways until you can no longer ignore them.

When you choose to engage fully with your high-value gifts, you might encounter challenges rooted in your programming, cultural conditioning, and what you've been told is "possible" for you. You might be afraid of your gifts, or think that they are too big for you to handle. Part of your task will be to break through these misconceptions in order to access your soul's truth.

Finally, the challenges you'll face when you really step into your superpowers and use them to the fullest of your abilities will show you the shadow side of your Wealth Code. When this duality reveals itself, it will be your choice which aspect to step into. The light side of your Wealth Code is aligned with your soul. The shadow side is aligned with your human ego, your fears, and your unresolved traumas.

But here's the beautiful thing: **If you find yourself in the shadow side of your Wealth Code, all you have to do is invite light into the shadow, and the shadow will retreat.** Like the half of the moon that is dark because it's facing away from the sun, the shadow side of your Wealth Code is just the part of your soul purpose and prosperity that needs to be illuminated.

The shadow side of your Wealth Code is the flip side of the coin. It's another set of tools you can use—but these tools are destructive and disempowering, instead of constructive and empowering. When we are in the shadow of our Wealth Code, we may feel disconnected, stressed, unworthy, or unable to deal with the challenge at hand. When we employ the tools of the shadow side, we blame, deflect, avoid, or attack our challenges instead of embracing them. In other words, we shrink instead of grow.

Once again, it comes back to our fear of the unknown. If we've just started to use our greatest gifts, or are recovering a superpower that we haven't accessed in a long time, our fears can push us into the shadow side of our Wealth Code, and trigger our deepest challenges around self-worth, love, acceptance, and visibility. Depending on our personal Wealth Code blueprint, we might become over-controlling, aggressive, self-destructive, or slip into "victim mode." We might believe others are to blame, or blame ourselves for not being good enough.

Given how busy, overstressed, overextended, and distracted many of us are to begin with, it's no wonder that we are tempted to avoid our challenges. A massive internal challenge on top of the daily grind can feel like the proverbial straw that broke the camel's back. And because we recoil from the challenge, instead of inviting it, the challenge never gets resolved. We actually end up spending *more* time with our feelings of fear and failure, because we're failing to meet our challenge.

Working through the challenges that your high-value gifts present is intense. It can be painful, and scary. Or, it can feel like you're standing at the foot of a huge mountain, looking up to the summit. You know you have to climb it, but you're totally unsure how to proceed.

Whatever you're feeling, know that the pain and fear don't last forever. In fact, once you start moving, climbing, and navigating your way up the trail, it probably won't seem so bad at all. Once you've scaled the mountain, you'll look back at the challenge, put together the puzzle pieces of how and why you struggled, and move forward with new knowledge and perspective. You might say something like, "Wow! If I had known *this* view was waiting for me, I would have climbed this bad boy a long time ago!"

The view, of course, is of your high-value gifts. The mountain was the gatekeeper to your greatness, the big test of your commitment to your own success. It was there to show you what you are made of, and prove to you—not anyone else, just you—that you are worthy of wielding your superpower.

On the other hand, pushing away our challenges keeps the pain and fear at a more manageable level, but it's a level that never goes away. You can try to find your way around the mountain, or under it, or through, but sooner or later, the terrain will get the better of you, and you'll have to start climbing. The more you fight it, the harder it will be.

The thing to remember when presented with mountainous challenges is this: there is always something in it for you, but you may not be able to see the gifts until the challenge is behind you.

MEET YOUR CHALLENGES, FIND YOUR WEALTH CODE

Katherine was a mother and naturopathic doctor with a successful practice. Her daughter had struggled with sensitivities from birth that the other doctors and practitioners could not figure out or help with. They would classify her with ADD or similar labels, but Katherine knew there was something deeper going on.

This was a very difficult situation for Katherine to deal with on her own, both because she knew there must be a better way to help her daughter, and also because her daughter was a challenging child to parent, and required a lot of extra time and attention. She felt very isolated and frustrated.

This situation was Katherine's mountain to climb—her soul challenge. Her search led her on a journey to discover new healing therapies to help her daughter and other ultra-sensitive children, as well as to create support systems for the parents of these children. In order to empower her daughter to thrive and use the unique gifts her extreme sensitivity bestowed, Katherine had to go beyond everything she'd been taught in medical school, and harness the intuitive and visionary superpowers she'd been born with.

Soon after she began this journey, the challenge got even bigger. As an empath and introvert, it was uncomfortable for Katherine to put herself in the spotlight and draw attention to her quest, but if she wanted to create the solutions she envisioned, she had to move past her fear. Her soul was calling her, loud and clear, to become more of who she already was in order to help her daughter.

She received the information that she needed to write a book to help parents in situations similar to hers, and teach them how to ask for and create the support they needed since they were unlikely to find it in traditional settings. Soon, she was teaching not only parents, but other intuitives and empaths, how to tap into the gifts of ultra-sensitivity.

Katherine's challenge was all about visibility. She was called to develop her confidence and self-assuredness so that she could step out as the intuitive visionary teacher she personified in her Sacred Wealth Code. She needed to be able to carry that level of confidence in order to lead the way for others into new territory, new ways of thinking, and new ways of being, and help them to uncover their own truths and visionary gifts.

How do you know if a challenge is a gateway to one of your greatest gifts—a soul challenge—or something created because you didn't listen to your soul? You feel it! It's the difference between climbing your mountain and hitting it with a stick—and it's vital to learn to recognize that difference, so you don't spend your precious time and energy pushing against something you can't change (like someone else's destructive life choices, or a soul-sucking job that doesn't engage your gifts).

To figure out what challenges will serve you (and which won't), tune into your heart. Say, "If I tell myself the truth, what's in this for me?"

There is *always* something for you in soul challenges (although what that something is may not always be clear). There is no benefit in the challenges you create on your own by ignoring your soul. With practice, you will feel the difference clearly in your heart, mind, and body.

The only way to get to the other side of a soul challenge is to engage with it. The only way to get to the other side of a self-created challenge is to meet the soul challenge you've been avoiding.

Either way, the mountain will be there, waiting for you.

The Blessing of Threes

What do you do when break through a challenge only to find yourself presented with the exact same situation all over again?

If this happens to you, don't give up. This is your soul's way of testing you. It's the training course before the big mission, the place where you can exercise your newfound gifts and talents in a controlled environment. The more you practice using your gifts, the more you integrate them into your life. Soon, like anything else you train for, they will become reflexive. You'll integrate your gifts from your soul to the soles of your feet, and it will be yours forever.

In fact, there is a spiritual principle which states that things always come in threes. So if you scale your mountain only to find that you have two more to climb, don't let it get you down. The Divine is just giving you a practice run.

On the next page, you'll find a simple exercise to help you engage with your soul challenges.

Wealth Alignment Practice 7

Write your challenge on one side of a piece of paper. **Then, take a deep breath, settle into your heart, and ask, "What's in this for me? What are the possible gifts on the other side of this challenge?"**

Write everything that comes up on the opposite side of the paper.

Now, for each possible gift, ask yourself, "What is one inspired action I could take to support myself in stepping into this gift and using it right now?"

Next, tune into your fears. What are you actually afraid of? What do you think might happen if you engage with this challenge? What's the absolute worst-case scenario?

On a new sheet of paper, write down all the fears that are coming up for you—even if they seem silly. **Then, ask yourself, "Is this true? Or is it F.E.A.R.—False Evidence Appearing Real?"**

If your fear is true, you'll instinctually know what to do, just as you know to jump back onto the curb when you see a car speeding toward you. If it's not true (which is far more common) that is also great information to have, because now you can flip that false fear around and write down what's actually true.

FEAR, VULNERABILITY, AND YOUR SACRED WEALTH CODE

A lot of people want to stand up and stand out in the world. They feel like their souls are calling them to do something big, but they feel like they're wearing an invisibility cloak that's hard to take off. Maybe they've climbed their mountains and practiced their gifts, but haven't gotten any recognition from the outside world. Maybe they've been using some of their gifts for years, but in a quiet way, because they never received confirmation or encouragement around their efforts. Maybe they were simply put down too many times in the past.

Whatever the reason, shedding that invisibility cloak and shining their light feels painful and threatening. And so, even after they identify and start using their gifts, they slip into the shadow sides of their Wealth Codes to defend against this feeling of invisibility, instead of treating it like just another mountain to scale.

There can be a great deal of vulnerability involved in sharing your superpowers with the world. When you use your greatest gifts, you're putting your real self—your authentic, divine self—on full display. You're standing up at the top of that mountain, waving your arms, shouting, "Here I am!" Is it uncomfortable? Of course! But until you do this, you will always be living in some kind of shadow, close enough to your Wealth Code to see it, but too far away to step into it.

When you live from your Wealth Code, you will no longer be able to follow the leader, because there is no one else out there who is exactly like you. There is no one out there who can give you permission or confirmation, because no one is standing where you are standing. This is a good thing. It means that you can create your own movement. You can create a new product, a new line of thought, a new state of being—and you can honestly claim it's the best of its kind, because there is nothing out there like it. It's original.

Yes, it would be beautiful if our whole world and everyone in it supported us when we step into this space of originality. But since not everyone in the world is living from their Sacred

Wealth Code, we can't expect them to understand where we are. We simply have to do what we are called to do, and trust that we know, better than anyone else, what our souls have planned for us.

There is a great deal of strength in this kind of vulnerability. Being vulnerable means you're being open, and true to yourself. Yes, the world gets to see you—but *you* also get to see you, perhaps for the first time in your life. You will never know your greatest gifts fully until you face the challenge of being seen.

When you're willing to be seen, your gifts will also be seen, and you'll start to see them reflected back to you by others. You'll understand how you are making a difference in others' lives, and in the world.

If vulnerability and visibility are challenges for you, start small. Practice being open in a safe space, with people you trust and who accept you for who you are. Once you know what the experience of true openness feels like, you'll want to bring it forward into the rest of your life!

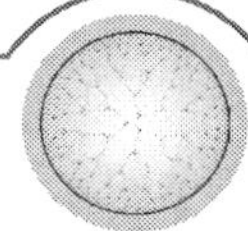

Wealth Focus

Reflection

Journal about or meditate on the following statement:

"If I tell myself the truth ..."

What challenges have I overcome in my lifetime?

What recurring challenges have I had to face?

What do I know about my soul challenges?

What is standing between me and my superpowers? How can I scale that mountain?

How do I feel about the challenges I uncovered in the exercises in this chapter? Am I judging them? How can I embrace them fully so I can tackle them with greater ease?

What happened the last time I fully engaged with one of my biggest challenges?

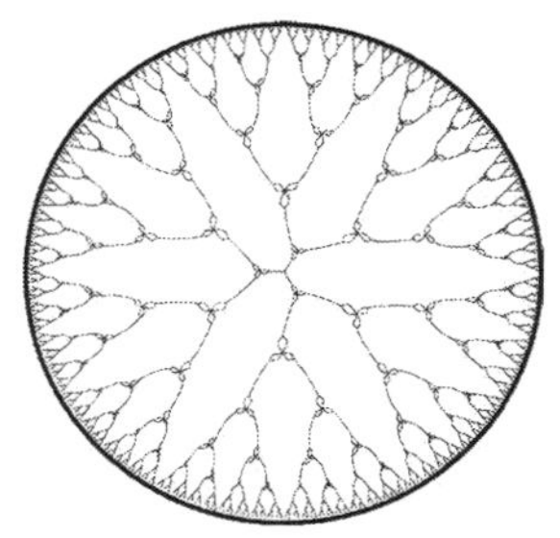

Part III

THE SACRED WEALTH ARCHETYPES

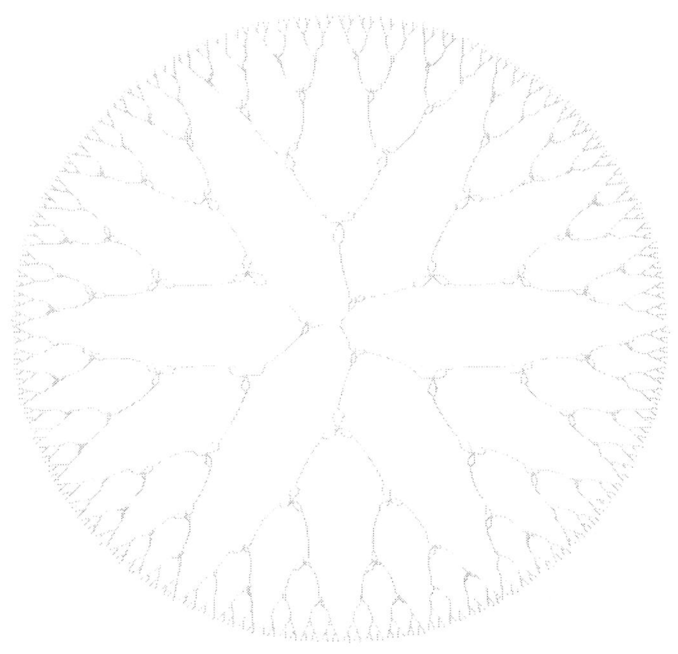

The Archetypes

Now that you have discovered the Four Pillars of the Sacred Wealth Code, and delved into what they mean and how they manifest for you, it's time to look through a different window into your Wealth Code: Your Sacred Wealth Archetypes.

Archetypal language is universal. Every culture, language, faith, and practice has its archetypes. They are a bridge between lofty concepts and energies and human experience. They speak the language of the soul.

We all have experience with archetypes, whether we know it or not. For example, when someone mentions a "warrior," you immediately understand the energy of that description. Same goes for a "teacher," "leader," or "muse." We experience archetypes through stories, cultural references, and even stereotypes. Each has its own story—a story which is so ingrained in our collective understanding that it needs almost no explanation. Archetypes unlock stories in ways that few other keys can do.

After years of studying Vedic Astrology charts and delving into the intersections of purpose and prosperity—the *dhana yogas*—which existed in each, I began to notice that archetypal energies were present. They were informed by the position and attitudes of the planets within each chart, but across thousands of charts, they were consistent. The more I studied them, the more loudly they spoke.

In Vedic Astrology, there is a mythology that goes along with each of the planets. These mythologies are built on archetypes which transcend cultural boundaries, and are every bit as relevant to modern Westerners as they were to the ancients of India. They allow us to insert ourselves into the stories of our individual soul blueprints, and understand the interwoven energies which make up our Sacred Wealth Codes.

The archetypal energies of the planets in your Sacred Wealth Code, and the area of your natal chart which contains your *dhana yogas,* speak volumes about your superpowers and high-value gifts. They speak the language of your soul. **When you meet the Sacred Wealth Archetypes, you will know them on a deep level. You will relate to them deeply and intimately, and see them as alive in your reality.**

As the Archetypes started to show up in the readings I was performing, I began to see how integrating them into my readings would help my clients move beyond intellectual understanding of what I was sharing, and into a deeper connection with their purpose, passion, gifts, and challenges—the pillars of their Sacred Wealth Codes. As I introduced the Archetypes to my clients, it was as if their high-value gifts and talents became instantly more available to them. Instead of trying to figure out how to integrate the knowledge I was sharing into their often chaotic daily lives, my clients simply had to embody and interact with their Archetypes to start using their superpowers and move closer to their soul neighborhoods. They could grow with their Archetypes until their energies were melded.

More, I began to understand and work with my own Archetypes—energies like The Magician, The Sage, and The

Teacher. The more I paid attention, the more they showed up! Soon, I was able to tune in with them, tap into their power, and rely on their guidance in my daily life and work. They led me even deeper into my Sacred Wealth Code, and helped me birth the potent body of work with which you are now engaged.

THE SACRED WEALTH ARCHETYPES

The Sacred Wealth Archetypes you'll meet in this section are the ones which were revealed to me through my research. Many may be familiar to you, either through your experience of Western astrology or through some other source. (I've used Western planetary names in the descriptions to help the Archetypes feel more relatable and accessible.)

What's important to remember as you familiarize yourself with these Archetypes is that they are new and different aspects of the archetypal characters with which you may be familiar. The Archetypes are immense, multi-faceted energies, and have many faces. The aspects presented here are filtered through the lens of your Sacred Wealth Code and *dhana yogas*—meaning, they specifically represent and relate to wealth and wealth creation via the intersection of purpose and prosperity.

Each of these Archetypes has its own set of "superhero" powers—high-value gifts which are found at the intersection of purpose and prosperity, and which relate specifically to attracting and creating wealth in the way you are divinely designed to do. Their energies, when integrated into your daily life, can help you bring the infinite energy of possibility into your reality through the practical application of your high-value gifts.

In other words, the Sacred Wealth Archetypes speak your soul language, and help you embody theirs. They already have one foot in your soul's vision of purpose, and the other in your soul's vision of prosperity. Their tool belts are stocked with superpowers, and their hands are full of high-value gifts. They are the keys to unlocking the story of your own wealth dream.

Your Archetypes can show up for you in an infinite number of ways. Once you acknowledge them, they are incredibly accommodating and personal. They are also timeless, ever-present, and ever-evolving. They are present on these pages in their essential forms, ready for you to invite into your life. You only need to meet them to know which are part of your soul.

A Note On The Sacred Wealth Archetypes and Your Personal Astrology

The Sacred Wealth Archetypes, as I've presented them here, are available for you to use in your life immediately. Read through the descriptions carefully, and take note of which archetypal "personalities" speak to you. Intuition is the most powerful tool you have for connecting with and embodying these essential energies. The more you work with the Archetypes, the more deeply they will align you with your Sacred Wealth Code.

Of course, there is no way for me to delve into your personal astrological chart in this format, and no way for me to effectively communicate the qualifiers that influence each Archetype depending on planetary positioning, the relationship of your Archetypes to the other planets in your chart, etc.* However, this does not diminish the powerful potential of the Archetypes to aid you in creating your wealth dream *right now*.

You don't need to understand every nuance of archetypal energy in your soul blueprint to start engaging with it. You simply need to be open to any and all information that comes through from your soul, and be willing to act on the knowing you receive. So as you read through the archetypal descriptions in the next

*If you are interested in learning more about these aspects in your astrological chart, I offer Sacred Wealth Code readings at www.SacredWealthCode.com.

section, be open to what comes through for you.

Ask yourself, "Does this Archetype speak to me? Can I relate to this Archetype? Does this Archetype hold a key to my Sacred Wealth Code?"

And, if the answer is yes, ask, "Is this Archetype part of my Sacred Wealth Code?"

Yes, identifying your personal Archetypes is that simple. Your soul knows the truth. All you have to do is listen.

HOW TO WORK WITH YOUR ARCHETYPES

It's time to dive in and meet your Sacred Wealth Archetypes!

On this journey, you'll want to bring with you all the knowledge, tools, and awareness you've gained so far in this book: your purpose, your "big why" for wealth, the passion that supercharges your purpose, your greatest gifts and talents, and your greatest challenges.

Armed with this knowledge, read through each of the Archetypes in the following section. Remember the lessons you've learned about using your intuition, and the way your body feels when something is resonant with your truth.

You will be drawn to certain Archetypes for different reasons. Sometimes, you will see your own passion and high-value gifts in the description, and know right away that, even if you don't fully embody those gifts right now, this Archetype holds a key to your wealth dream. At other times, you might find a reflection of your greatest challenge in the shadow side of an Archetype, and see the potential gifts on the other side of your current struggles.

As you read, mark all of the Archetypes that resonate with you. Write about them in your journal. Use the questions at the end of each Archetype's description to help you connect more deeply, and determine whether this Archetype is perfectly matched with your soul's desire for wealth and what you know about the Four Pillars of your Sacred Wealth Code.

All of the Archetypes in this section exist within you somewhere, but most people have only three to five of these distinct energies in the zone of their Wealth Code. It's okay if you identify with more than that, but once you create your initial list of resonant Archetypes, take extra time to sit with each one. Be sure that you're not passing judgment on an Archetype based on a pre-existing idea of what makes a King, an Engineer, or a Nurturer. (Remember, these are the wealth faces of these Archetypes, so they may manifest differently than you expect.) Also, be sure you're not choosing an Archetype based on wishing, or wanting to be different than you are. Wishing to be someone else, or wishing for a different set of high-value gifts, won't get you closer to your Wealth Code or the fulfillment of your purpose; in fact, it will move you further away. So for every Archetype that makes your initial list, tune in with your soul and sit with your true feelings before deciding if that Archetype is really part of your Wealth Council.

Once you have chosen your Wealth Council—the set of Archetypes that speak most clearly to your soul, and with which you will work going forward—it will be time to put those energies to work for you and start manifesting your wealth dream. In Chapter Eight (which appears after the Archetype descriptions), I'll share exactly how you can work with the Archetypes that have spoken to you. You'll learn how to channel their energies in your daily life, ask them for help when you need it, and add their superpowers to your own toolkit to manifest wealth through your purpose, passion, gifts, and challenges.

If you take this work to heart, and really embody the Sacred Wealth Archetypes to which you will connect in this next section as well as the Four Pillars you discovered in Section II, you will be propelled along your soul's wealth path in a way you never believed possible.

Enjoy this deep dive into your soul's truth! I'll see you on the other side.

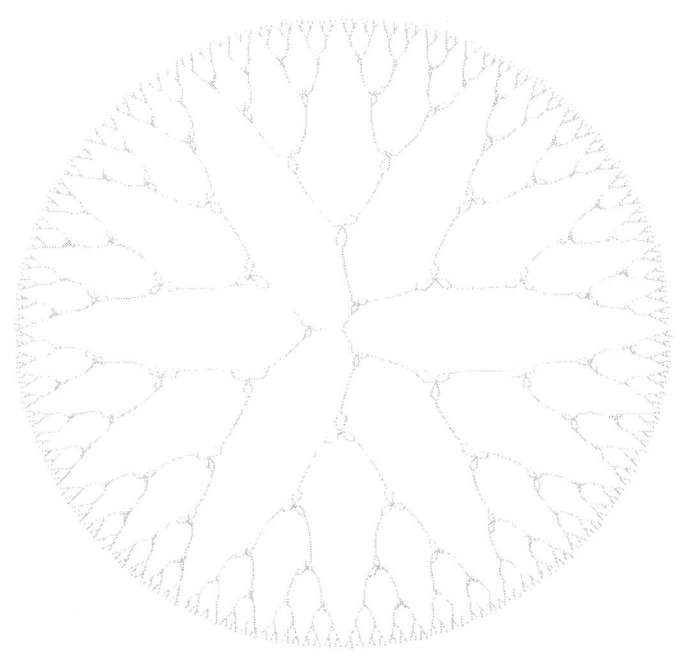

The Archetypes

QUICK PAGE REFERENCE

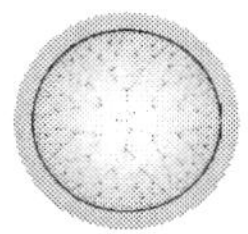

The Leader

(Sun)

CONFIDENT. BRILLIANT. PURPOSEFUL.
COURAGEOUS. COMMITTED. AUTHENTIC.
POSITIVE. INSPIRING. PASSIONATE. EMPOWERED.
VISIONARY. VITAL. INTEGROUS. TRUSTWORTHY.

MANTRA: "I lead from the heart."

SOUL DESIRE: To live up to your highest potential and guide others to theirs for the greatest good of all.

PURPOSE: To live in the present, free from the past, and to create an ideal future.

SHADOW: Arrogant. Narcissistic. Addicted to power. Over-controlling.

The Leader is an inspiring, confident, purposeful person with the clarity to courageously lead others toward a better future.

As a Leader, you embody the true essence of leadership, in that you guide by example and teach others to lead themselves. You have a vision; therefore, you can help others create a vision, and inspire them to align with your goals. You're in authentic partnership with the Divine and the world, and are often known as a CEO, consultant, director, president, spiritual leader, thought leader, parent, coach, mentor, entrepreneur, teacher, trainer, manager, team leader, planner, recruiter, chief, or executive. You are found in every profession and walk of life.

You are brilliant, heart-centered, and lead from the inside out by tapping into divine guidance, trusting your intuition, and being an authentic expression of your most valued gifts and talents. You are passionate about developing people, and know that true fulfillment comes from genuinely being valued. You expertly build a secure structure where your team is using their most valued gifts to achieve more than they believe is possible while contributing to the success of the whole. You've united them, and now they are committed to moving your mission forward as if it was their own.

As a Leader you are present, soul aligned, flowing with new ideas, and on the leading edge of your movement. You have the superpower of solving complex problems; you always know just what to do and how to do it. You find soul satisfaction in taking matters into your own hands, leaning into challenges, and becoming the solution to the problem. You often work harder than everyone else, and you always do the right thing, even when it's difficult or unpopular.

You are humble, put others first, are willing to serve, and have the superpowers of deep listening, inspiring others, and empowerment. You are attuned to a higher potential for all and believe in a shared mission and success, so you guide people to places where they would not go alone.

The Shadow of The Leader

You are better than most at what you do, but if you let it go to your head your ego will stroke you into arrogance. Unfortunately, you'll believe that you are better than everyone, and that all beings are below you. This puts a big chasm between you and your team, and breeds serious mistrust.

If fear has its grip on you, you've lost your connection with the Divine. You can become addicted to power—and, like other addicts, can delude yourself into thinking that more is always better. You'll become a workaholic, your inspiration will dry up, and you'll isolate yourself—especially if your mindset shifts to a point where both power and responsibility feel like yours and yours alone.

When you are stressed, you can be over-controlling. When this happens, it may feel impossible for your team to trust you or be led by you. You will literally squeeze the life out of your mission.

If you find yourself in the shadow of The Leader, you've lost your connection to the source of your being and put your ego in charge. It's time for a serious break to get back to the roots of whatever spiritual practice keeps you tuned in and present. Take a personal retreat, travel, or do something fun and creative to help you realign and reconnect with your purpose and mission before returning to work.

High-Value Gifts

- Presence
- Problem Solving
- Has a big vision
- Authenticity
- Decisive
- Listens
- Creates a supportive environment for success
- Consistent and trustworthy
- Leads by example
- Clearly communicates
- Inspires others to action
- Sees others' strengths
- Magnetizes alignment with mission

Inspired Action Plan

"I practice presence to be divinely aligned with my high-value gifts and live into my greater potential while courageously leading others to theirs."

Tapping In with Your Leader

Consult with your Leader by meditating and journaling on the following questions to activate your unique high-value gifts and talents.

- What are my Leader's high-value gifts and talents?
- How can I use these high-value gifts and talents in my current work or the work I want to be doing?
- What is one inspired action I can take today to do that?

Coming Out of The Shadows

- What aspects of The Leader's shadow energy are present in my life right now?
- How does this shadow energy affect my connection to and expression of my divine purpose?
- What is one inspired action I can take today to release this shadow energy?

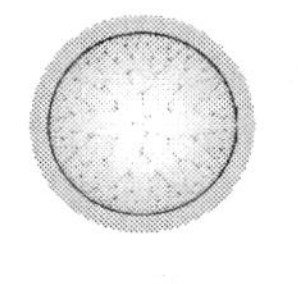

The King

(Sun)

REGAL. POWERFUL. PASSIONATE. COURAGEOUS. SOVEREIGN. RESPONSIBLE. BENEVOLENT. CREATIVE. INNOVATIVE. DECISIVE. DIRECTIVE. INSPIRING. VISIONARY. RESPECTED.

MANTRA: "I powerfully lead my mission."

SOUL DESIRE: To expertly use power for higher order, growth, and security.

PURPOSE: To excel at creating a resilient and wealthy business, community, or organization.

SHADOW: Dictator. Over-controlling. Greedy. Entitled. Isolated.

The King is a luminous, regal, empowered, and soulful leader who is in pursuit of excellence in all things. Known as the CEO, spiritual leader, president, politician, authority, commander, judge, superintendent, executive, controller, supervisor, or chief, he is in complete charge of his domain and expertly drives it to a higher level of prosperity and success.

As a King, you're sovereign, creative, and autonomous in the way you live and lead your life and mission. You're on a quest with a big vision, and nobly take full responsibility for the success of your endeavors. You're rich in worldly knowledge, but receive your ultimate direction from the Divine. Your superpower is leadership, and you take a stand for a higher order to create positive change, growth, and security for your kingdom.

You're highly valued for your brilliance, ability to solve complex problems, and expertise in producing results. You powerfully drive yourself and those you lead to achieve higher goals. As soon as you reach the top of one mountain, you've already devised and executed a plan of action to conquer the next. Because you know the essence of a true leader is to teach others to lead, you always have a strong and trusted administration to help you implement your plan for achieving your mission.

You're potently tapped into the currency of universal power, and use it to manifest and receive spiritual and material wealth. You're inherently generous, and love to share. Security for the future is important for you and your people, so protection of people and resources is built into your overall plans.

Kings magnify their brilliance and power by being well-connected. You excel at developing strategic relationships that help carry out your mission.

The Shadow of The King

You're committed to excellence, but sometimes you can slip into entitlement and greed. When this happens, you become a self-serving dictator. Fearing you will lose power, money, or control, you become self-centered. You get too attached to money and personal gain, misuse your power and your people, and eventually fall from grace. Your administration loses trust in you as you hurt those you care about and who are essential to the success of your mission.

If stressed, you can forget the true essence of leadership and become over-controlling. This leads you to disempower your administration by over-ruling and micromanaging them. But, since it's impossible to achieve your goals without your team, this is actually detrimental and can lead to the total demise of your success.

It can be lonely at the top. Because you are so concerned about creating security for the future, you forget to be present and enjoy what you have now. All work and no play will leave you feeling isolated and alone—so don't be afraid to get out there and party with the commoners every once in a while!

High-Value Gifts

- Strong Leadership
- Courageous
- Powerful
- Long-range vision
- Dependable
- Creates positive change and growth
- Excels in chosen field
- Shines in the public eye
- Solves complex problems
- Gets desired results
- Provides security
- Knows how to create and implement a successful plan

Inspired Action Plan

"I tap into the higher power of Spirit to guide me in the pursuit of excellence. I use my high-value gifts to benevolently lead my mission for the greater good of my people."

Tapping In with Your King

Consult with your King by meditating and journaling on the following questions to activate your unique high-value gifts and talents.

- What are my King's high-value gifts and talents?
- How can I use these high-value gifts and talents in my current work or the work I want to be doing?
- What is one inspired action I can take today to do that?

Coming Out of The Shadows

- What aspects of The King's shadow energy are present in my life right now?
- How does this shadow energy affect my connection to and expression of my divine purpose?
- What is one inspired action I can take today to release this shadow energy?

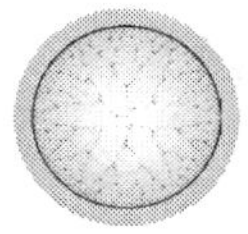

The Celebrity

(Sun)

CHARISMATIC. IMAGINATIVE. LUMINOUS. CONFIDENT. AUTHENTIC. INSPIRING. PASSIONATE. MAGNETIC. IMPACTFUL. PUBLIC. FASHIONABLE. INDEPENDENT. NOBLE. GENEROUS. UNIQUE.

MANTRA: "I lead with my light."

SOUL DESIRE: To use the power of radiance to lead and uplift others.

PURPOSE: To uniquely shine my light to lead a successful mission and movement in the world.

SHADOW: Overdramatic. Drama Queen. Self-centered. Egocentric.

The Celebrity is a charismatic, inspiring, and luminous leader who is a powerful trendsetter. As a Celebrity, you were born to shine your radiance into the world. You are often known as an actor, entrepreneur, politician, public figure, model, leader, or famous personality.

You have a dignified presence and alluring mystique, and can attract wealth by being a superstar on the stage of your life and business. Like a rose blooming in the sun, you thrive in the limelight and in front of an audience. You value luxury, are fashionable, and acquire adornments that help you sparkle in your chosen field while you passionately take a stand for the cause, idea, or product you are championing.

You have the high-value currency of luminosity. You naturally project an image of success, and create an impact by creatively attracting attention and notoriety to yourself and your movement. Your unique genius is illuminating solutions to challenging or complex problems. You're generous, and enjoy being a spokesperson for charities near and dear to your heart.

As a Celebrity, you are driven by freedom of expression. This also means that you love to make a big, often dramatic, impression. You need to be seen on a platform that serves your purpose, and are always looking for ways to bring your biggest vision to your audience.

Big goals and high expectations—for yourself and for others—are part of your makeup. Your brilliance inspires others to be their best selves, and you do your best work when you are at the helm of a team, company, or organization where you can operate with complete creative license.

The Shadow of The Celebrity

You are the blazing sun at the center of your own solar system, and this self-focus serves you in many ways—but if your ego takes the lead, you can become self-centered and arrogant, and forget that other planets even exist. You lose your generosity and ignore the needs of your team as you spiral into a self-serving mission. When your mission no longer uplifts the world, you have betrayed your faithful followers, and they will abandon your ship, leaving you unsupported as you eventually crash and burn.

Every Celebrity needs a stage where he or she can show up and shine. In order to positively obtain the attention you seek, you need to establish a productive way to be visible through your business, art, or profession, and use that visibility to serve a greater good. If you don't, you will slip into the energy of the Drama Queen, and make it all about you instead of all about what you stand for in the world. This unnecessary drama and over-complication of situations will quickly wear out the people you depend on.

If you find yourself in the shadow of The Celebrity, you are cut off from the Divine. Perhaps you are feeling insecure, or are leading from your head without your heart. No matter what the cause, it's vital for you to take the time to reconnect with your radiance and the greater mission that truly inspires you, so you can show up and shine in your truest glory.

High-Value Gifts

- Authentic leadership
- Creative expression
- Good director
- Inspires others to be their best selves
- Shines radiance that uplifts others
- Entertains to bring joy
- Leads by example
- Role model
- Creative problem solving
- Self-motivated

Inspired Action Plan

"I connect my head with my heart and authentically use my high-value gifts to show up on my stage, shine my glorious light, and successfully lead my movement in the world."

Tapping In with Your Celebrity

Consult with your Celebrity by meditating and journaling on the following questions to activate your unique high-value gifts and talents.

- What are my Celebrity's high-value gifts and talents?
- How can I use these high-value gifts and talents in my current work or the work I want to be doing?
- What is one inspired action I can take today to do that?

Coming Out of The Shadows

- What aspects of The Celebrity's shadow energy are present in my life right now?
- How does this shadow energy affect my connection to and expression of my divine purpose?
- What is one inspired action I can take today to release this shadow energy?

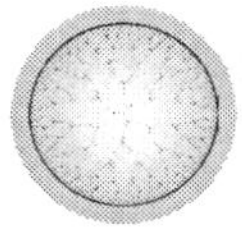

The Great Nurturer

(Moon)

MOTHERLY. NURTURING. DEVOTED. LOVING. WISE. EMPATHETIC. COMPASSIONATE. ABUNDANT. GENEROUS. RECEPTIVE. EMOTIONAL. INCLUSIVE. SUPPORTIVE. STABLE.

MANTRA: "I give and I receive nourishment."

SOUL DESIRE: To be a channel for unconditional love, abundance, and growth.

PURPOSE: To nurture growth and create community.

SHADOW: Over-giving. Martyrdom. Over-emotional. Over-attached.

The Great Nurturer is a mother, teacher, humanitarian, supporter, coordinator, gardener, problem solver, counselor, caregiver, and healer. When you embody this Archetype, you are deeply in touch with the life pulse of humanity and the planet. You're a conduit for unconditional love, patience, caring, and nourishment.

Your first priority is to give substance and sustenance where it's needed to nurture life. You know you're on purpose when you're fulfilling your deep need to be of service. You feel truly fulfilled at the end of the day when you know in your heart that you've made a difference for someone.

You are highly sensitive, feel the needs of the masses, and thrive on connection. You intuit what others need in order to grow and develop to the next level. You're gifted with the knowledge of what to give to others so they can grow on their own terms, and refrain from disempowering them by doing it for them. You feed the roots of the tree, so that its branches may grow strong and abundant.

You have a special gift for bringing people together, and can create your own flourishing community. This also makes you highly valuable to leaders and organizations, because you create a supportive culture that attracts the right people while growing the soul and mission of the business.

As a Nurturer, you are a creatrix—a feminine creator. Like Mother Nature herself, what you touch and pour your love into grows vibrant and strong. You tend the garden of life. Therefore, it is essential that you act as the creatrix in your own life first and foremost, and create your soul's calling. Otherwise, you can err on the side of helping others too much with their projects, and put too little energy into your own.

The Shadow of The Great Nurturer

If you are playing the Martyr—moaning about how much you do for others, and that no one does anything for you—then you are stuck in over-giving. You feel obligated to give to others, and believe that you have no choice but to do what's "expected" of you. This results in feelings of resentment, anger, and isolation.

You're intensely connected to your feelings, and care profoundly for the people in your life. However, when you carry the burden of other people's pain, the pain of the masses, or the pain of the planet, you lose touch with your divine connection. You can become over-emotional and even depressed.

If you find yourself in the shadow of The Great Nurturer's energy, you are seriously undernourished. It is time to feed your body, heart, and soul by eating life-giving foods, reading something soul-inspiring, working on your own projects, and spending time with dear ones who give you the love you need. Only when you feel filled up again should you do anything for anyone else.

High-Value Gifts

- Respectful
- Responsible
- Practical
- Collaborative
- Connective
- Reliable
- Loyal
- Attractive to others
- Sees the best in people

Inspired Action Plan

"I nourish my body and soul first, so I may abundantly use my high-value gifts to nurture others with exactly what they need to grow and do for themselves."

Tapping In with Your Great Nurturer

Consult with your Great Nurturer by meditating and journaling on the following questions to activate your unique high-value gifts and talents.

- What are my Great Nurturer's high-value gifts and talents?
- How can I use these high-value gifts and talents in my current work or the work I want to be doing?
- What is one inspired action I can take today to do that?

Coming Out of The Shadows

- What aspects of The Great Nurturer's shadow energy are present in my life right now?
- How does this shadow energy affect my connection to and expression of my divine purpose?
- What is one inspired action I can take today to release this shadow energy?

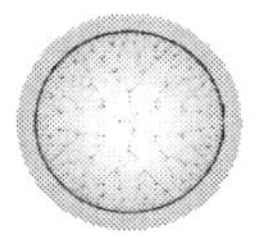

The Queen

(Moon)

REGAL. COURAGEOUS. PROSPEROUS. LOYAL. POWERFUL. COMPASSIONATE. INTUITIVE. RESPONSIBLE. ADMINISTRATIVE. KNOWLEDGEABLE. TRUSTWORTHY.

MANTRA: "I am an empowered feminine leader."

SOUL DESIRE: To wield power for positive growth and order.

PURPOSE: To create a successful and prosperous business, community, or family.

SHADOW: Unable to delegate. Being a dictator. Self-righteous. Tyrannical. Over-controlling.

The Queen is a wise, radiant, regal, and empowered divine feminine leader who is wise beyond her years. She is known as the boss, leader, CEO, politician, role model, manager, and public figure. She is on a mission, fully in charge of her domain; she knows the needs of her people and how to best lead them.

The Queen knows her value, and is potently tapped into the essence of prosperity. She enjoys the finer things in life with great reverence and appreciation. She is admired and respected as a courageous and loving leader, and is always comfortable on the big stage.

As a Queen, you take a stand for sovereignty in the way you lead and live your life. You are in touch with your authentic purpose, and regally take responsibility for it. You are tapped into the collective consciousness, and your mission reflects what is good for the collective. You are politically savvy and are skilled at dealing with public affairs.

You have a big vision for your mission that requires the service of others. One of your superpowers is to shine your light on the people that serve your mission, and bring out the best in them. You earn your team's loyalty, trust, and devotion.

Queens are well-connected, and understand that while *what* you know is important, *who* you know is equally important. Your connections with the right people help you get things done quickly and easefully. Order is the upside of control; you're a master of order, and skillfully take charge of establishing it. You have the capacity not only to see a vision, but also to see how it will be obtained. You take responsibility for the order in your domain.

The Shadow of The Queen

You are dedicated to achieving and obtaining the best of everything, but sometimes you can slip into being self-serving. This will make you into a control freak, because you want things done your way—and *only* your way. Or, you may lose the ability to delegate, because you don't think anyone else can do it as well as you can.

If you are feeling self-righteous or acting like a dictator, you are taking yourself far too seriously. You've forgotten your dignity. You may be the leader, but it's not all about you. If you stay stuck in this energy it will become a self-fulfilling prophecy. You will eventually lose your devoted team, and be left alone to do everything by yourself.

If you find yourself in the shadow of The Queen's energy, you are depleted and have become selfish. It is time to replenish your energy, so indulge in some lavish self-care, reestablish your divine connection, and get intimate with the essence of your mission by remembering why it's important to *you*.

High-Value Gifts

- Leads from the heart
- Perceptive
- Generous
- Uplifts the masses
- Has a big vision
- Protects others
- Shines in the public eye
- Influences collective change

Inspired Action Plan

"I honor my value and use my high-value gifts to confidently, compassionately, and nobly lead my mission to success."

Tapping In with Your Queen

Consult with your Queen by meditating and journaling on the following questions to activate your unique high-value gifts and talents.

- What are my Queen's high-value gifts and talents?

- How can I use these high-value gifts and talents in my current work or the work I want to be doing?
- What is one inspired action I can take today to do that?

Coming Out of The Shadows

- What aspects of The Queen's shadow energy are present in my life right now?
- How does this shadow energy affect my connection to and expression of my divine purpose?
- What is one inspired action I can take today to release this shadow energy?

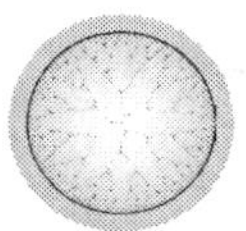

The Collaborator

(Moon)

COOPERATIVE. RECEPTIVE. CONNECTIVE. SUPPORTIVE. CURIOUS. EMPATHETIC. RESPONSIBLE. INSIGHTFUL. ACCEPTING. INCLUSIVE. RELIABLE. CO-CREATIVE.

MANTRA: "I co-create to create."

SOUL DESIRE: To use your unique genius in connection with others to actualize a vision or goal.

PURPOSE: To create greater good for the global community through authentic partnership.

SHADOW: Needy. Scattered. Overcommitted. Overworked. Over-loyal.

The Collaborator is intimately connected to the power of "we," and is a great partner, team builder, colleague, coworker, associate, and assistant.

As a Collaborator, you are a relationship builder who is curious, cooperative, and flourishes as part of a team. You work well in authentic partnerships to bring ideas and projects into fruition for the greater good. You imagine a world where everyone is focused on using their unique genius, and doing what expands and cultivates a collective vision.

Collaborators feed off of the exchange of ideas to manifest a vision, project, or goal. You have the power to mastermind, and do your best work serving as high council to others. You know the indispensable value of a team where everyone is focusing on using their high-value gifts, and believe that the collective succeeds most brilliantly when everyone is focused on doing their part.

You are an integral part of a vision that is greater than your own; you are secure and confident in knowing that we are all greater together, and that you do not need to do it alone. Because you're inclusive, you shine by sharing the high-value currency of your unique gifts in collaboration with others, and are profoundly satisfied when operating as a part of a succeeding team.

Although you are a team builder, you also excel at leading your part of the greater vision. You're reliable, and it's very clear to others that they can count on you to do your part. You know exactly what you're in charge of, and you take charge of it. You act as the "governor" of your part of a project, and loyally execute that part to completion, all while keeping in mind the greater vision of the whole, and the activities of others in the production court.

Even when you're focused on your own projects, you still work best in collaboration with others. You're highly relational; you dig working with other people. If on a solo journey, you can feel cut off and isolated—like you're marooned on a deserted island. When working with others, you feel like a shining link in a valuable chain; whether you or another is creating the exquisite pendant which will hang from it, you are still part of the resulting beauty.

The Shadow of The Collaborator

When your Collaborator becomes needy, it's because you are not getting the recognition you need and deserve as a valuable part of the team. You may be on the wrong team, but feel afraid to make a change or leave a project or job. Your colleagues may want you to be the "workhorse," and take on tasks that you are merely good at, rather than the ones you are exceptional at. Yes, you have an intense need to belong, and work best in authentic partnership—but you shouldn't fear moving on from a team that is not valuing your unique genius.

Your need to be part of a team can lead you to become overly committed and overly loyal. When you don't get the recognition you deserve, you simply try harder. The problem with this approach is that you can work yourself into the ground in the hope of being seen and valued. But, chances are, when you're burned out, exhausted, and miserable, your unique genius is nowhere to be found.

If you're scattered or are questioning every move you make, you have lost your connection with yourself and the greater vision of what you are working on. Without the joyful focus through which you bring projects to completion, you may find yourself spinning in circles. Or, you may become so involved with other people's projects that you lose sight of your own place in the grand scheme.

If you find yourself in the shadow of The Collaborator, it's time to step back, reconnect with your purpose and soul desire, and evaluate if those you're working with are recognizing your high-value gifts. Surround yourself with people who love and appreciate you, and you'll soon be back on your game.

High-Value Gifts

- Co-creator
- Authentic partner
- Committed
- Insightful
- Team player
- Allows others to shine
- Focused on your part of the greater goal

Inspired Action Plan

"I develop my unique genius while remaining connected to the power of 'we,' and focus on using my high-value gifts to co-create with others in service of a bigger vision."

Tapping In with Your Collaborator

Consult with your Collaborator by meditating and journaling on the following questions to activate your unique high-value gifts and talents.

- What are my Collaborator's high-value gifts and talents?
- How can I use these high-value gifts and talents in my current work or the work I want to be doing?
- What is one inspired action I can take today to do that?

Coming Out of The Shadows

- What aspects of The Collaborator's shadow energy are present in my life right now?
- How does this shadow energy affect my connection to and expression of my divine purpose?
- What is one inspired action I can take today to release this shadow energy?

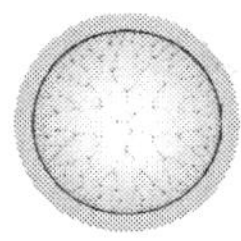

The Communicator

(Mercury)

TRUTHFUL. OUTSPOKEN. FLEXIBLE. CLEAR. QUICK. RELATABLE. FRIENDLY. INTELLIGENT. OPEN-MINDED. INTUITIVE. PSYCHOLOGICAL. DISCRIMINATING. INFORMED. PROCESSING. ARTICULATE.

MANTRA: "Words have power."

SOUL DESIRE: To be a channel for clarity and growth.

PURPOSE: To speak the truth, and illuminate clarity and understanding for the positive growth of humanity.

SHADOW: Overwhelmed. Sarcastic. Blunt. Pessimistic.

The Communicator knows the power of words to educate, inform, uplift, grow, transcend, open possibilities, and connect to the truth. Communicators gather, process, and share information to help uplift humanity.

Communicators are process-oriented and found in all walks of life and professions. As a Communicator, you may be known as a psychologist, counselor, writer, facilitator, mediator, comedian, interpreter, editor, PR person, social media expert, salesperson, or astrologer. **Your word is as good as gold, and you expertly use it to share ideas, information, and concepts which help others evolve and grow.**

You are friendly, open, clear, direct, and connected to divine truth. All forms of verbal and nonverbal language are your currency. You are gifted with the universal language of metaphor. You have the unique genius to distill and synthesize complex subjects, broad themes, and big-picture ideas, and make them easily understood. This is healing and transformative for others.

You're also gifted with the mindful, Buddha-like energy of discernment and discrimination. This helps you break attachments to what no longer serves, positively re-frame difficult situations, and move on to whatever life has to offer next. This gift is of highest value when you serve others in their growth and development.

You have the superpower of deep listening, and can hear and address the true message of what's being said, even when the speaker is stifled in their expression. You speak from the heart, and can put words to things others can't. You facilitate finding common ground and creating unity.

The Communicator knows a lot of people, and is an innate networker. You can greatly profit from your alchemical genius of putting information, people, and things together in brilliant ways that no one else has considered before.

The Shadow of The Communicator

If you are in the shadow energy of the Communicator, your words can be blunt, like cudgels, or razor-sharp sarcastic with the power to cut another down. Your words can do more harm than good. If you don't check yourself, you can hurt those you love and care about.

If you are unfocused, multi-tasking too much, or involved in too many projects, you will end up overwhelmed. Trying to process too much at once leaves you all over the map, and not achieving any of your goals.

When stressed, you mentally spin, and are negative and pessimistic. You're in a fog, and don't see or translate things clearly. This leads to major breakdowns in communication, and painful misinterpretations and misunderstandings.

If you find yourself in the shadow of The Communicator, you have too many plates in the air, or are trying to be too many things to too many people. It's time to take some personal time to quiet your mind with meditation, deep relaxation, and time in nature; once you reboot your mindfulness and restore your clarity, your brilliant mind will put everything in order once again.

High-Value Gifts

- Clarity
- Mindfulness
- Reliability
- Flexibility
- Discernment
- Deep listener
- Gifted writer
- Gifted speaker
- Mental brilliance
- Catalyst for growth

Inspired Action Plan

"I am committed to practicing presence and mindfulness so I can continue to grow and dedicate my high-value gifts to serve the growth and evolution of humanity."

Tapping In with Your Communicator

Consult with your Communicator by meditating and journaling on the following questions to activate your unique high-value gifts and talents.

- What are my Communicator's high-value gifts and talents?
- How can I use these high-value gifts and talents in my current work or the work I want to be doing?
- What is one inspired action I can take today to do that?

Coming Out of The Shadows

- What aspects of The Communicator's shadow energy are present in my life right now?
- How does this shadow energy affect my connection to and expression of my divine purpose?
- What is one inspired action I can take today to release this shadow energy?

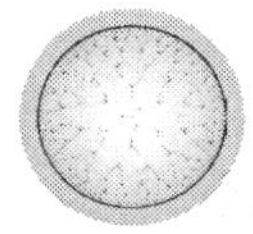

The Merchant

(Mercury)

LOGICAL. DISCERNING. FLEXIBLE. FINANCIAL. PSYCHOLOGICAL. CREATIVE. COMMUNICATIVE. SOCIAL. BRILLIANT. QUICK. EVALUATIVE. TECHNICAL. INVENTIVE.

MANTRA: "Opportunities to prosper are everywhere."

SOUL DESIRE: To be a creative channel for prosperity.

PURPOSE: To accumulate wealth to provide for the material needs of your people.

SHADOW: Workaholic. Moody. Materialistic. Greedy.

The Merchant is a brilliant, discerning, and flexible transactor who is conscious of the abundant possibilities for creating prosperity in the world. As a Merchant, your goal is to accumulate wealth and provide for the material needs of people. Your soul purpose demands that you create wealth by being in service to others.

As a Merchant, you work well in any profession that caters to the masses. You may be known as a salesperson, executive, entrepreneur, transactor, advertiser, negotiator, consultant, banker, stockbroker, business coach, copywriter, venture capitalist, techie, or digital marketer.

You are aware that everything in the universe has an energetic currency. You're an expert evaluator, and quick to quantify the value of resources and information in order to discern how they can best be channeled for trade, commerce, and profit. Like a great chef, you're marvelously inventive, and possess a unique genius that allows you to put a new spin on the resources at hand and create something new to present to the world for a prosperous outcome.

A business-minded master networker, you are always on the lookout for opportunities to connect people, ideas, and assets in order to bring a potentially lucrative project to life. You're a hard worker, and tend to multi-task; you almost always have several plates spinning at a time. Your keen instincts allow you to make quick decisions, and your adventurous spirit drives you to push the edges of tradition when it comes to sales and trade. Because you're tapped into infinite possibilities, you take the necessary risks to make the deal happen—and, even when it doesn't, you know the next big opportunity is right around the corner.

You are emotionally intelligent and a skilled conversationalist, and have the high-value currency of connection. You tend to have a positive outlook, and are all about "living the good life." You love sharing resources with others and the world, and inspire other people to enjoy the parts of life which matter most to them. By artfully connecting the positive emotions that people want to have with your chosen product or service, you create success for all parties involved.

The Shadow of The Merchant

You have a lot of ideas and are a very hard worker by nature. You believe that time is money, and can easily slide into workaholism by indiscriminately chasing all the opportunities around you. However, all work and no play will drive you over the cliff of overwhelm and burnout.

You're flexible and sensitive, and are therefore usually good at handling change—but when you're trying to handle too many changes at once, you get stressed, and can become very moody and hard to deal with. When your emotions get the best of you, you won't be able to close a deal, which of course will make your bad mood even worse.

You are programmed to prosper, but if you get sidetracked by making money for the sake of money alone, you'll get caught in the nasty net of materialism and greed. When this happens, you may put things before people; this will rob you of your relationships. You'll be way off-purpose because your prosperity will no longer be connected to serving others. In the end, you'll have money, but you'll be all alone. Remember, money can buy some things, but it can't buy love or happiness.

If you find yourself in the shadow energy of The Merchant, you are cut off from your divine purpose, and caught in the trap of believing that you alone are the source of profit in your world. It's time to take a break from work to reboot your connection with the source of your being and your greater purpose. Commit to "living the good life" here and now: spend time with loved ones, and enjoy the prosperous relationships and connections you've already created.

High-Value Gifts

- Great evaluator
- Creative thinker
- Business-minded
- Good negotiator
- Great at making deals and sales
- Networks well
- Embraces change
- Willing to take risks
- Trusts instincts
- Quick to recognize new opportunities

Inspired Action Plan

"I am committed to honing my high-value gifts to create wealth while being present to the needs of the many, so I can contribute and give back to the world."

Tapping In with Your Merchant

Consult with your Merchant by meditating and journaling on the following questions to activate your unique high-value gifts and talents.

- What are my Merchant's high-value gifts and talents?
- How can I use these high-value gifts and talents in my current work or the work I want to be doing?
- What is one inspired action I can take today to do that?

Coming Out of The Shadows

- What aspects of The Merchant's shadow energy are present in my life right now?
- How does this shadow energy affect my connection to and expression of my divine purpose?
- What is one inspired action I can take today to release this shadow energy?

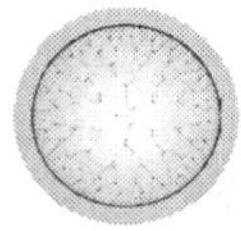

The Messenger

(Mercury)

PERCEPTIVE. PROGRESSIVE. INTELLIGENT.
ADAPTABLE. CHANGEABLE. PSYCHIC. CLEVER.
VERSATILE. CANDID. AGILE. COMMUNICATIVE.
INSIGHTFUL. IMAGINATIVE. CURIOUS. INSTINCTIVE.

MANTRA: "I bring the light of awareness."

SOUL DESIRE: To be an interpreter of the divine mind.

PURPOSE: To translate and deliver news and truths which wake others up to new perceptions and a higher level of being.

SHADOW: Scattered. Selfish. Fickle. Uncommitted. Confused.

The Messenger is a perceptive, intelligent, and versatile interpreter who delivers the truth or news that others most need to hear. **The Messenger acts as a versatile bridge between the three domains of mind, body, and spirit.**

Messengers are masters of both the spoken and written word, and can be found in all walks of life. As a Messenger you may be known as a mediator, guide, agent, courier, emissary, astrologer, ambassador, forerunner, minister, herald, advisor, reporter, liaison, negotiator, attorney, representative, or storyteller. Your potent and eloquent way of communicating is intended to alter others' consciousness so they can awaken and evolve to a higher level of being.

You are candid, amiable, insightful, good-humored, and well-connected to the road of consciousness. All forms of language are your currency. You are a gifted storyteller who creatively delivers truthful messages at precisely the right times, and know how to set the stage so that your wisdom doesn't fall on deaf ears. You are a divine scribe who knows that the pen is mightier than the sword, and have the unique genius to artfully translate the soul languages of scriptures, dreams, archetypes, and ancient texts, so that humanity can understand their divine wisdom and easily discover the personal value they hold. This can literally be life-changing for others.

As a Messenger, you shine the light of awareness through the news you deliver. You awaken people, communities, and organizations to the truth so they can more effectively mobilize their energy and efforts in order to reach their goals and fulfill their missions. You are flexible, and have the high-value gift of streaming information from the creative and logical minds simultaneously. This makes you an excellent negotiator and "middle man" who brings things to a fruitful conclusion for all concerned.

You are greatly valued for your natural adaptability, as well as for your ability to track information on multiple levels while staying on course. Where others would easily get lost or distracted, you can navigate the way to your intended outcome. You are a gatekeeper of perception on the path to integrating mind, body, and spirit, and have the unique genius to blend and amalgamate information to create new pathways and opportunities for others.

The Shadow of The Messenger

If you are in the shadow energy of the Messenger, you can become scattered and stuck in confusion about what's true and what's not. You might have difficulty making sense of what you see and hear, and so your thoughts might go from being like a golden thread of truth to feeling like a tangled, useless ball of string. This inner entanglement leaves you tongue-tied, frustrated, and unable to deliver a clear message.

If you are stuck in your head, multi-tasking too much, or not adequately attending to your body and spirit, you will become unbalanced and separated from your purpose. Trying to function from the neck up is like firing on only one out of three cylinders, and it will cut you off from your greater brilliance. If you let yourself become too worn down, you will stall out. This can lead you to disappoint the people who rely on your wisdom and clarity, or even give up on your mission entirely.

When stressed, you are fickle and selfish. You change your mind constantly, and this may lead others to think you can't be trusted. Your light of awareness grows dim, and you become a messenger of negativity instead of positive growth. This can leave you sad, isolated, and blocked.

If you find yourself in the shadow of The Messenger, you are stretched too thin, unbalanced, and cut off from the divine mind. It's time to draw your energy inward and replenish your mind, body, and spirit. Meditate, read inspirational or spiritual books, get some bodywork, exercise, make love, and spend time in nature. Once you replenish all three levels of your energy, you will return to balance, and your light of awareness will shine brightly once more.

High-Value Gifts

- Highly perceptive
- Skilled translator
- Negotiation
- Good-humored
- Insightful
- Good communicator
- Talented speaker
- Talented writer
- Wakes people up to the truth
- Creates new opportunities
- Mobilizes others into action
- Flexible and adaptable

Inspired Action Plan

"I am committed to living in balance with body, mind, and spirit so I can give my high-value gifts to serve others in awakening to a higher level of being."

Tapping In with Your Messenger

Consult with your Messenger by meditating and journaling on the following questions to activate your unique high-value gifts and talents.

- What are my Messenger's high-value gifts and talents?
- How can I use these high-value gifts and talents in my current work or the work I want to be doing?
- What is one inspired action I can take today to do that?

Coming Out of The Shadows

- What aspects of The Messenger's shadow energy are present in my life right now?
- How does this shadow energy affect my connection to and expression of my divine purpose?
- What is one inspired action I can take today to release this shadow energy?

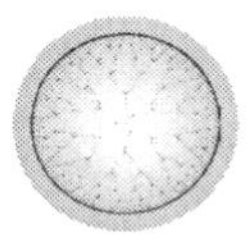

The Connector

(Venus)

HEART-CENTERED. INTIMATE. CREATIVE. COMMUNICATIVE. DIPLOMATIC. DEVOTED. HARMONIOUS. INSPIRING. ACCOMMODATING. RECEPTIVE. COMPASSIONATE. EMPATHETIC.

MANTRA: "We are all One."

SOUL DESIRE: To be a channel for eternal belonging-ness.

PURPOSE: To be a centralizing force for humanity, and bring the world together.

SHADOW: People-pleasing. Loss of self. Overly attached. Codependent. Too comfortable.

The Connector is a sensitive, heart-centered person whose primary desire is to be in deep connection to self, Source, and others.

As a Connector, you are a finely-skilled relationship artist who is often known as a counselor, networker, diplomat, teacher, or human relations specialist. You put a high value on relationships, and have a unique ability to meet people exactly where they are with intimacy, compassion, and understanding.

The Connector is keenly aware that we're all divinely connected. As a Connector, you're at home and flourish in the company of others, and your actions remind us that we are all one. You're social, community-oriented, and a natural networker. You have a wealth of relationships, and communication is your currency. You are gifted with a deep well of inspiration that gives you the golden threads of connectivity to weave together people with people, people with opportunities, and people with themselves.

You have an inherent magnetism that draws others to you, and makes them immediately comfortable in your presence. People quickly open up to share their innermost desires and challenges with you. You are like a warm, safe haven for people in need.

Connectors are harmonious beings, and get along well with others. You have the high-value gift of empathy, and easily feel the needs of other people, animals, plants, and the world around you. Because you tap into the essence of things, you often see or feel directly into the heart of what's going on beneath the surface. You also have the valuable gift of problem-solving; you see how sometimes unlikely things fit together, and seek to connect others with the best possible solutions.

Your gift of communication is extremely valuable, and you can profit by authentically relating to others using your innate gifts of compassion, understanding, and inspiration. You are diplomatic, and a centralizing force for humanity; your superpower is bringing the world together. You are fascinated with human drama, and seek to inspire the cast of characters in the play of your life to be their best selves.

The Shadow of The Connector

If you are people-pleasing, it's because you want everyone to be happy—but also because you want to be liked, which is simply not possible all of the time. Underneath your smiles, you're afraid of losing love and security, and being left alone. When you feel insecure, you become self-negating and overly attached to people and outcomes. This leaves you feeling unseen, misunderstood, powerless, and often ineffective toward your goals. You can also stay in harmful or debilitating relationships long past their prime.

Because you are empathetic and can connect so intimately with others, you can lose yourself and become codependent unless you maintain a strong spiritual anchor. In fact, you may take on other people's energy and problems like they are your own without even knowing it! When this happens, it is because you're misinterpreting what love truly is, and feel like you need others to need you in order to feel loved. This is painful, and flat out soul-squashing. Neediness will wear you out, blind you to the goodness in life, hijack your dreams, and leave you mired in drama.

Connectors like luxury and comfort, and can err on the side of remaining attached to comfortable things—jobs, material goods, and relationships—instead of stepping into their full potential.

If you find yourself in the shadow of The Connector's energy, you're giving too much of what others want, and not enough of your true high-value gifts. It's time to come back home to your divine connection, and put your personal and spiritual needs first. Spend some time in nature or on a retreat to get intimately reacquainted with your purpose and mission before returning to service.

High-Value Gifts

- Good networker
- Inspiring
- Relational
- Creative communicator
- Highly connective
- Spiritually connected
- Creates a sense of belonging
- Intuitively knows what others need and want

Inspired Action Plan

"I connect with myself, Source, and then others. When I do this, I can effectively use my high-value gifts of inspiration and communication as my currency to remind others that relationships are a reflection of divinity."

Tapping In with Your Connector

Consult with your Connector by meditating and journaling on the following questions to activate your unique high-value gifts and talents.

- What are my Connector's high-value gifts and talents?
- How can I use these high-value gifts and talents in my current work or the work I want to be doing?
- What is one inspired action I can take today to do that?

Coming Out of The Shadows

- What aspects of The Connector's shadow energy are present in my life right now?
- How does this shadow energy affect my connection to and expression of my divine purpose?
- What is one inspired action I can take today to release this shadow energy?

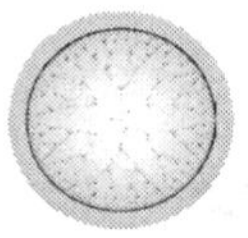

The Artist

(Venus)

CREATIVE. VISIONARY. IMAGINATIVE.
IDEALISTIC. CONNECTIVE. HARMONIOUS.
PASSIONATE. RECEPTIVE.
REVERENT. SPIRITUAL.

MANTRA: "I create my visions."

SOUL DESIRE: To creatively express yourself and connect with others through your creations.

PURPOSE: To manifest beauty in the world.

SHADOW: Undervaluing yourself. Perfectionism. Unchecked idealism.

The Artist is a creator, inventor, innovator, musician, dancer, performer, writer, or visionary. As an Artist, you have a deep reverence for beauty and can see it almost everywhere. You are inspired by the beauty in the world, and you express the wealth of your visions through your art to uplift the world.

Your primary motivation is to create. Your viewpoint is unique, and needs to be channeled through your chosen medium to full expression in order for you to realize your value. You walk to the beat of your own drummer, and listen to your intuition; you are "inner-referenced." Because you see from the inside out, you're a master of inspired action, and have the ability to make your inspirations a reality that others can see, feel, hear, or touch. You're well-liked and naturally connective, and have a magnetism which enhances your power of attraction; you draw people to you through your creations.

As an Artist, you dwell in your right brain, where you have a plenitude of creative ideas. Typically, you take a non-traditional approach in your work, and love to forge new ways of doing things. One of your superpowers is to weave ideas and mediums together in new ways. This makes you a valuable resource of creative solutions for logistical, left-brained thinkers.

The Shadow of The Artist

If you are undervaluing yourself, chances are you have a core belief that you are not enough, or not good enough. You were most likely programmed with this belief at an early age by parents, teachers, or peers, simply because these people shared their opinions about you and your artwork. This mindset can undermine your efforts to make money and create wealth from your art.

When you are in the shadow of the Artist, you may see such an idealized vision of what you want to create that you become disappointed—even devastated—when your practical efforts at creation don't match the ideal. When you focus on the faults in your work, or get caught up in perfectionism, you block your creative genius from doing its magic. You might abandon projects before they're complete—or, worse yet, never even start that next great work of art.

If you find yourself in the shadow of The Artist, it's important to get back in touch with your purpose, move

your body to get out of your head, spend time in nature, and surround yourself with people who appreciate you and your work.

High-Value Gifts

- Imaginative
- Curious
- Unique perspective
- Able to see from multiple viewpoints
- Eye for beauty and aesthetics
- Power of attraction
- Intense focus

Inspired Action Plan

"I hone my artistic high-value gifts to create my visions through my chosen artistic medium."

Tapping In with Your Artist

Consult with your Artist by meditating and journaling on the following questions to activate your unique high-value gifts and talents.

- What are my Artist's high-value gifts and talents?
- How can I use these high-value gifts and talents in my current work or the work I want to be doing?
- What is one inspired action I can take today to do that?

Coming Out of The Shadows

- What aspects of The Artist's shadow energy are present in my life right now?
- How does this shadow energy affect my connection to and expression of my divine purpose?
- What is one inspired action I can take today to release this shadow energy?

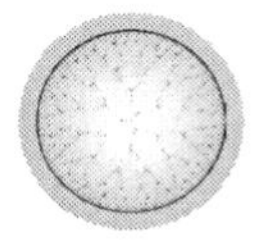

The Muse

(Venus)

INTUITIVE. INSPIRED. IDEALISTIC. CREATIVE. DIVINELY-CONNECTED. PASSIONATE. EMOTIONAL. SENSITIVE. EMPATHETIC. MAGICAL.

MANTRA: "I inspire, and I am inspired."

SOUL DESIRE: To be a channel for creativity and genius.

PURPOSE: To make life a form of art.

SHADOW: Inner critic. Control issues. Scattered. Lack of follow-through.

The Muse is the creative voice of the soul. If you are working with the Muse Archetype, you have a direct connection with divine inspiration.

As a Muse, you are here to manifest your truth in co-creation with the universe and others. Your purpose and mission is to make life a form of art. You are smart, creative, and sensitive. You have your own personal style and authentic stance, which you express through your work in the world.

The Muse in you is an introvert by nature. You can easily shut out the external noise of the world to hear the creative whisper of your soul. You are a divine interpreter who sees the creative genius that may be invisible to others.

You are an exceptional collaborator who gives inspiration and clarity to, and facilitates growth in, all those whom you encounter. You understand the inner dialogue between the Self and the soul, and are highly valuable to others as a channel to their soul's creativity. One of your superpowers is to help those around you breathe life into their dreams. Essentially, through your own natural process, you support others in living their purpose through the creative expression of their own gifts, reconnect them with their own genius and talents, and assist them in bringing their next profitable idea down to earth.

The Muse needs to be worshipped and adored. When she is, she will appear on call to pour her ingenious nectar into your next great idea for your business, art, or collaboration. When she is feeling unloved, however, she can become fickle, or disappear for long periods of time—so it's essential to take time every day to listen to and follow her guidance.

The Muse is essential to creation, but may appear only fleetingly for those for whom she is not one of their Sacred Wealth Archetypes. Being a Muse, you know how to court her when she becomes elusive for others. You frequent the soul-inspired highway of ideas, and are familiar with all the back roads and on-ramps. You're rarely at a loss for where to find the next great idea. That makes you one of the best collaborators that an artist, entrepreneur, or leader can have.

The Shadow of The Muse

The Inner Critic is the voice that doubts, judges, and criticizes the Muse's unseen gifts. The Inner Critic seeks to control. Control is fear dressed up in logic, and seeks to squelch the Muse's inspiration.

When you are in the shadow of the Muse, you may not trust yourself and your unseen gifts. You may let other people's opinions rob you of your innate knowing, or feel unable to follow through on your divinely-inspired ideas. Jumping from one project to the next, frustrated and anxious, you may fail to bring anything to completion or reap the rewards of your creative work.

If you find yourself in the shadow of The Muse, it's important to take some time to get quiet and go within, so you can hear the voice of your soul louder than the ranting of your inner critic or the opinions of others.

High-Value Gifts

- Inspired Genius
- Imaginative
- Channel for others' creative ideas
- Visionary
- Collaborator
- Original Thinker

Inspired Action Plan

"I quiet my mind and open to my high-value gifts of soul inspiration to co-create my truth with the universe and others."

Tapping In with Your Muse

Consult with your Muse by meditating and journaling on the following questions to activate your unique high-value gifts and talents.

- What are my Muse's high-value gifts and talents?
- How can I use these high-value gifts and talents in my current work or the work I want to be doing?
- What is one inspired action I can take today to do that?

Coming Out of The Shadows

- What aspects of The Muse's shadow energy are present in my life right now?
- How does this shadow energy affect my connection to and expression of my divine purpose?
- What is one inspired action I can take today to release this shadow energy?

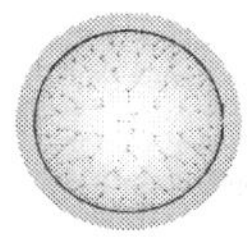

The Honorable Warrior

(Mars)

BRAVE. COURAGEOUS. STRONG. PASSIONATE. BOLD. HARDWORKING. TERRITORIAL. LEADER. ATHLETIC. COMPETITIVE. DECISIVE. HEROIC. LOYAL. DISCIPLINED. ACTION-DRIVEN. HIGH-ENDURANCE.

MANTRA: "I take a stand for positive change."

SOUL DESIRE: To pursue personal excellence and world change through courageous acts.

PURPOSE: To stand for honorable causes that evoke your strengths and be an agent for positive change.

SHADOW: Rescuer. Narcissistic. Volatile. Self-neglecting.

The Honorable Warrior is empowered with confidence, courage, determination, and drive to be a champion for worthy causes and create positive change in the world.

As an Honorable Warrior, you are a strong, brave, passionate, hardworking, loyal, action-oriented spiritual warrior who is guided by a higher power. You're known as a protector, athlete, boss, executive, soldier, advocate, liberator, defender, lawyer, politician, champion, or hero. You're in tune with the balance of power between light and dark, and are willing to fight the good fight for a cause in which you strongly believe. You will stand for the underdog when they can't stand for themselves, and are at your best when you're saving the world.

As the Honorable Warrior, you are perpetually in the pursuit of personal excellence, and are most fulfilled when protecting those you care for while taking a stand for a noble cause. You have the enduring passion to achieve your heart's desires, and the focus, will, and ambition to reach your goals. You have the superpowers of ambition and motivation, and can light a fire under others that motivates them to reach for their goals.

You're a good leader, independent, and in full charge of your domain. You can take action on your own while being part of a greater cause or organization, but you also know the power of interdependence, and that it takes a team to achieve the largest goals. You thrive when surrounded by comrades, and have a wealth of inspiration for your brothers and sisters to be a little braver (and up their game through healthy competition) as you continually take your life and ambitions to the next level.

The Honorable Warrior is known as a driving force. You're disciplined, and know that "where there's a will, there's a way." You take great pride in any mission you're involved in, so when representing another's mission, you're viewed as an invaluable asset because you will take action as if it were your own.

You have the high-value currency of productivity. You "just do it," and get things done. You're highly valuable to any project or organization you're a part of.

The Shadow of The Honorable Warrior

The Honorable Warrior will go on a rescue mission when it is truly needed, but can sometimes fall into the negative pattern of the Rescuer. The Rescuer has misguided attachments, and needs to be needed to feel worthy.

If you're playing the part of the Rescuer, you are refusing to see the divine wholeness in others; instead, you see only their weaknesses. You need a Victim to rescue to feel valued and loved. This can lead to codependency and disempowerment for both the Rescuer and Victim.

Because you sometimes let ambition get the best of you, and tend to work even harder when times are tough, you tend to neglect yourself. This will leave you stressed, burned out, and cut off from divine guidance. Your narcissistic tendencies will then emerge, and you may end up compromising your values to "win," or use control to get what you want at any cost. This must be avoided, as it is highly detrimental not only to you, but to all concerned.

If you are not actively fighting a good and worthy fight in the world, you can become highly volatile and engage in aggressive behavior—even to the point where you cause harm to those you love. You need to be wary of becoming addicted to confrontation, as you will eventually alienate yourself as well as those around you.

If you find yourself in the shadow of The Honorable Warrior, your ego has edged out the Divine. You replenish and reconnect best through right action, so it is time to reinstate a regular exercise program that will make you sweat regularly and take the edge off your ambition. You should also reconnect with proper mentorship to guide you in your purpose, and recommit to a daily spiritual practice.

High-Value Gifts

- Willfulness
- Strength
- Courage
- Ambition
- Motivation
- Leadership
- Productivity
- Conviction
- Creates change
- Pursuit of excellence

Inspired Action Plan

"I honor and follow divine direction to be empowered with my high-value gifts, commit to a worthy cause, and wholeheartedly serve to create positive change in the world."

Tapping In with Your Honorable Warrior

Consult with your Honorable Warrior by meditating and journaling on the following questions to activate your unique high-value gifts and talents.

- What are my Honorable Warrior's high-value gifts and talents?
- How can I use these high-value gifts and talents in my current work or the work I want to be doing?
- What is one inspired action I can take today to do that?

Coming Out of The Shadows

- What aspects of The Honorable Warrior's shadow energy are present in my life right now?
- How does this shadow energy affect my connection to and expression of my divine purpose?
- What is one inspired action I can take today to release this shadow energy?

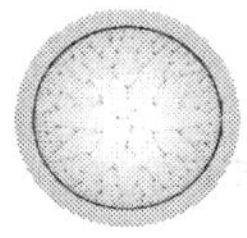

The Engineer

(Mars)

CURIOUS. PRODUCTIVE. TECHNICAL. HARDWORKING. FOCUSED. CREATIVE. COMPETENT. PRACTICAL. COMPETITIVE. DECISIVE. DETERMINED. ANALYTICAL. ADVENTUROUS. LOYAL. GENEROUS.

MANTRA: "Every problem has a solution."

SOUL DESIRE: To be a channel for discovering a better way.

PURPOSE: To discover and apply better paths of action for positive change in the world.

SHADOW: Negative. Self-judging. Arrogant. Aggressive. Over-analytical.

The Engineer is fascinated by what makes things tick, and is highly gifted when it comes to designing better solutions to all of life's issues.

As an Engineer, your approach to life and work is curious, creative, practical, technical, logical, and focused. You are determined to solve problems and design new ways of getting the results you desire. The brilliance of The Engineer can be seen everywhere in the world. You improve the way we live, work, travel, communicate, stay healthy, build things, care for the environment, market, entertain, and uplift the world. You are found in all trades and professions.

You're inherently curious, and have the high-value currency of bettering, fixing, adjusting, altering, and solving everyday problems. You are deeply satisfied by exploring the inner workings of things. You're an enthusiastic researcher, and readily absorb information to be analyzed; then, you put your creative spin on your analysis in order to design the best solution. You are highly valued as the logical, perceptive, and discriminating go-to person to solve the problem at hand, create a practical design for a new idea, or to discover a better way to get the job done. You are never short of puzzles to solve.

As an Engineer, you are a master of energy—and your energy must be productively channeled. You process information as an introvert, but express it as an extrovert. Being spiritually aligned is of utmost importance to your self-discipline, as well as your ability to abundantly create and prosper on the material plane.

You're hardworking, competent, and dedicated to getting results. You are indispensable to Visionaries (and Visionary companies) because you can take an idea and create the practical nuts and bolts necessary to make it a reality and put it to good use. You're independent by nature, but manifest best in the company of others as the leader of a team.

The Shadow of The Engineer

If you're not grounded and attuned with your body, you are probably over-analytical and stuck in your head with a disregard for emotions—including your own. You become frustrated and arrogant, full of "shoulds" and judgments to make other people wrong. You can also become overly aggressive. This is detrimental to problem-solving, especially when those problems include the human equation. When you go into this place, your relationships will suffer.

When you are stressed, you can become negative, self-judging, and overly analytical. You get "stuck in your head," running the same negative thought loops over and over, unable to make a decision to save your life. Your work and health will suffer.

If you find yourself in the shadow of Engineer energy, you are spiritually cut off. You are stuck in your head, and your ego has taken over. It is time to get a spiritual reboot by getting grounded in your body through physical activity and being in nature, so you can remaster your energy and get back in touch with your purpose and mission.

High-Value Gifts

- Problem solving
- Critical thinking
- Determination
- Hard worker
- Technical
- Trustworthy
- Focused on results
- Gifted designer
- Practical application of ideas

Inspired Action Plan

"I maintain my spiritual connection to guide my high-value gifts of problem solving and designing to create a better future for all."

Tapping In with Your Engineer

Consult with your Engineer by meditating and journaling on the following questions to activate your unique high-value gifts and talents.

- What are my Engineer's high-value gifts and talents?
- How can I use these high-value gifts and talents in my current work or the work I want to be doing?
- What is one inspired action I can take today to do that?

Coming Out of The Shadows

- What aspects of The Engineer's shadow energy are present in my life right now?
- How does this shadow energy affect my connection to and expression of my divine purpose?
- What is one inspired action I can take today to release this shadow energy?

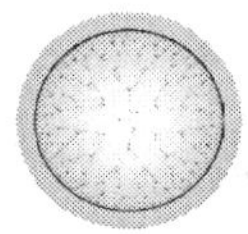

The Strategist

(Mars)

HIGH-ACHIEVING. PRODUCTIVE. SMART. CALCULATING. PASSIONATE. STRONG. DECISIVE. AMBITIOUS. ENTHUSIASTIC. SYSTEMATIC. COMPETITIVE. ACTIVE. CONVICTED. TACTICAL. GOAL-ORIENTED. PERSISTENT. GRITTY.

MANTRA: "Every vision has a plan."

SOUL DESIRE: To be a channel for planning, producing, and formulating better ways to realize a worthy mission.

PURPOSE: To help visions become successful missions through inspired action plans.

SHADOW: Self-centered. Over-competitive. Perfectionist.

The Strategist is a success-driven individual with the profound desire to support future growth. As a Strategist, you are highly gifted when it comes to devising strategic plans which align vision with action to create a better world.

You are ambitious, smart, passionate, decisive, technical, and on a path of personal precision. You're often known as an architect, entrepreneur, technician, politician, boss, manager, CEO, militarist, planner, brander, designer, athlete, coach, salesperson, auditor, analyst, legislator, director, developer, agent, or tactician.

The work of Strategists can be seen everywhere in the world. You help to create a better future by empowering great thought with the deliberate, purposeful actions which create results.

You're an instinctive groundbreaker and have the high-value currency of planning, designing, organizing, and charting future developments that meet the needs of progress. You take your inner direction from the divine mind, and turn it into outer direction in the world. You are outcome-oriented, and find finishing projects and achieving your goals deeply rewarding. You're at home on the leading edge of future development, skillfully armed with the necessary data and always ready to take action. Your passion for improvement keeps the wheels of your calculating mind turning, and you're always mapping new methods and systems to improve outcomes and bring plans to fruition.

As a Strategist, you are a masterful, innovative leader who has the unique genius of merging big-picture vision with strategic direction. You can create the necessary forms and functions for all types of projects, businesses, and organizations to succeed. You're hardworking and agile, work well under pressure, and are a keen problem solver. Your out-of-the-box thinking makes it possible to get the job done even when events throw a wrench in the works.

You are artfully calibrated to the energy of creation and production. Self-reliant, self-motivated, and trustworthy, you're a natural entrepreneur, but also a treasure chest of value to purpose-driven organizations and companies. You will prosper in a position that gives you the freedom to move according to your own internal vision and direction, while still serving a greater mission.

The Shadow of The Strategist

Because the first steps of your greatest work are constructed in the privacy of your mind, at times you may get locked away in the castle of your mind with the key nowhere in sight. If you start seeing yourself as a legend in your own mind, you can easily become arrogant and self-centered. When this happens, it's easy for you to forget that you're on a higher mission. Your ego will take over, edging out the Divine and the voice of your soul, and your carefully-constructed projects and teams will crumble.

When you're stressed, you can become ungrounded, lose touch with your body, and forget to exercise. Your over-calculating mind will kick into high gear, and relentlessly drive you toward perfectionism. This need to be better and better will soon overshadow your truly great work. You'll think yourself in circles instead of being productive and moving forward. Frustration and irritability will set in, and you will be too tangled in your what-ifs to implement your brilliant plans.

If you're off purpose, your ambition can get the best of you, causing you to trade in your healthy competitive edge for aggression and chest-thumping. This causes conflicts instead of successes, burns bridges, and cripples your mission.

If you find yourself in the shadow of Strategist energy, you are cut off from the divine mind. Your ego is ruling your world. It is time to reconnect with your body through regular exercise, competitive or outdoor sports, and meditation or prayer. Remember why you are doing what you're doing, and realign your body, mind, and spirit with your greater purpose and mission.

High-Value Gifts

- Decisive
- Purpose-driven
- Productive
- Leader
- Self-directed
- Out-of-the-box thinker
- Technical
- Outcome-oriented
- Achieves goals
- Plans methods and systems

Inspired Action Plan

"I maintain my divine connection so as to be guided by a higher power to employ my high-value gifts, create action plans to execute successful projects and missions, and create positive change in the world."

Tapping In with Your Strategist

Consult with your Strategist by meditating and journaling on the following questions to activate your unique high-value gifts and talents.

- What are my Strategist's high-value gifts and talents?
- How can I use these high-value gifts and talents in my current work or the work I want to be doing?
- What is one inspired action I can take today to do that?

Coming Out of The Shadows

- What aspects of The Strategist's shadow energy are present in my life right now?
- How does this shadow energy affect my connection to and expression of my divine purpose?
- What is one inspired action I can take today to release this shadow energy?

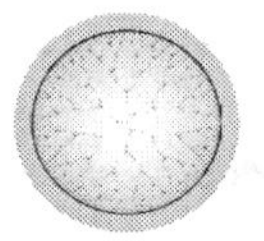

The Teacher

(Jupiter)

KNOWLEDGEABLE. INTELLIGENT. GROWTH-ORIENTED. TRUSTABLE. UNDERSTANDING. COMMUNICATIVE. COMPASSIONATE. PROSPEROUS. SOCIAL. INSPIRED. SELF-AWARE. GENEROUS. CONSIDERATE. VIRTUOUS.

MANTRA: "To know is to grow."

SOUL DESIRE: To illuminate and artfully communicate knowledge which uplifts humanity.

PURPOSE: To be a conduit for learning, growth, and change in the world.

SHADOW: Arrogant. Craves recognition. Overconfident. Manipulative. Controlling. Know-it-all.

As a Teacher, you are a creative communicator who believes that to know is to grow. Your desire is to share your knowledge, wisdom, experience, or skills with others.

You're highly intelligent, kind, social, generous, and deeply dedicated to supporting others in the achievement of their goals. In addition to being a teacher, you may also be known as a mentor, coach, professional, lawyer, team leader, trainer, tutor, advocate, or counselor.

You recognize that you are a conduit for learning and growth, not the source of it. You are aware of the high-value currencies of understanding and communication, and have a unique ability to "turn on the light bulb" for others. You're aware that people process information in different ways, and are masterful at simplifying complex concepts. You find creative ways to relate information so that your students can absorb, embody, and make practical use of the knowledge.

You're a voracious learner, and have a wealth of knowledge to draw from. You can teach on many subjects. The Teacher understands that the "what" and "how" of a subject are not enough to keep students interested; they need to understand the "why" in order to fully embody the knowledge you are imparting, and remain engaged through the sometimes-challenging process of learning.

Teaching is a superpower that is not exclusive to formal schooling; it is valuable in all areas of life. Learning is what helps every person reach their higher potential. As a Teacher, you are a co-creator with the Divine, and a conduit to uplift humanity by providing the nourishment of knowledge that every mind, body, and soul needs to grow to the next level.

You attract new teaching opportunities by following your own hunger to learn more of what inspires you. You're trusted by many, and can profit greatly through your generosity of giving what you know to whoever needs it—on or off the job.

The Shadow of The Teacher

If you don't remember to put on your oxygen mask first and practice good self-care, you can burn out from supporting others.

When you lose your connection with the divine, you may begin to believe that you know it all, or that you are the source of knowledge rather than simply the conduit. This leads to an arrogant, high-and-mighty way of being, and the need to be right while making others wrong. Such actions will, ultimately, cause you to fall from grace and lose the respect that others once had for you.

When you are stressed and attached to outcomes, you may have a tendency to try to control or manipulate others for your own benefit. This is soul-crushing for all parties involved.

If you find yourself in the shadow of The Teacher, you are probably stressed, burned out, and far from being a divine co-creator for learning and growth. It's time for you to have some fun, and rejuvenate with a soul-inspiring retreat that will reconnect you with the source of your being.

High-Value Gifts

- Knowledgeable
- Connective
- Good communicator
- Inspiring
- Practical
- Wise
- Supportive
- Strong mentor
- Trustable
- Strong presence

Inspired Action Plan

"I align with higher knowledge to nourish and grow myself first, and then use my unique genius of teaching to compassionately and generously serve others."

Tapping In with Your Teacher

Consult with your Teacher by meditating and journaling on the following questions to activate your unique high-value gifts and talents.

- What are my Teacher's high-value gifts and talents?
- How can I use these high-value gifts and talents in my current work or the work I want to be doing?
- What is one inspired action I can take today to do that?

Coming Out of The Shadows

- What aspects of The Teacher's shadow energy are present in my life right now?
- How does this shadow energy affect my connection to and expression of my divine purpose?
- What is one inspired action I can take today to release this shadow energy?

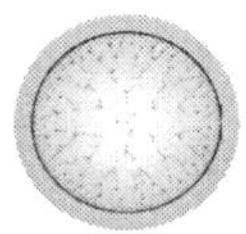

The Visionary

(Jupiter)

INVENTIVE, EXPANSIVE, WISE, INSIGHTFUL, ENTHUSIASTIC, CURIOUS, COURAGEOUS, PHILANTHROPIC, IMAGINATIVE, WEALTHY, KNOWLEDGEABLE, CONCEPTUAL, INSPIRED, IDEALISTIC, BENEVOLENT, HUMBLE.

MANTRA: "The world is filled with possibilities."

SOUL DESIRE: To manifest future possibilities in the present to uplift the world.

PURPOSE: To illuminate possibilities and create a vision for the greater good.

SHADOW: Hubris. Overexpansion. Overly idealistic. Lack of action. Perfectionism.

The Visionary has the insight and wisdom to tap into higher potential and create innovative solutions for the greater good of all.

As a Visionary, you are attuned to the big picture, and are often known as an inventor, entrepreneur, consultant, designer, director, lawyer, writer, traveler, or mystic. **You are both an introvert and an extrovert. You absorb information from the world, intuitively process it, and intellectually express your ideas.**

You have an enlightened perspective and excel at anything that truly interests you. You're an igniter, and your contagious enthusiasm for the next great vision readily attracts the support of others. A humanitarian at heart, you're most inspired by projects that uplift humanity and achieve a collective goal.

You are idealistic, courageous, and optimistic, and live in a world of possibilities. Ideas are your currency, and you easily invent creative solutions on the spot. You're curious and imaginative, with the superpower of improvisation. Problems and challenges are soul-satisfying opportunities for you to channel and implement your next brilliant idea. This makes you a highly-valuable advisor, counselor, consultant, or guide.

As a Visionary, you're attuned to divine guidance and see the interconnectedness of all things. You're an independent, free thinker, and—much like a computer processor—you think in systems. You can synthesize multiple data points at once, and can greatly profit from your ability to quickly illuminate new possibilities, solutions, and plans that are beyond the horizon of most people's vision.

The Shadow of The Visionary

When stressed, the Visionary is plagued by perfectionism. You focus on the minor details that are not as important to the big picture, and therefore struggle to bring things to completion. You become overly idealistic, and are deluded in trying to measure your efforts against the impossible.

Hubris can get the best of you when you get caught in egotistical thinking. When you become self-centered, you can forget that it takes collaboration to bring a vision to fruition.

You're a big thinker, but more is not always better. You can become "too big for your britches" when you are ungrounded and cut off from Divine guidance; this can lead you to expand your ideas to the point of ruin. You can lose money, your vision—even your loved ones.

If you find yourself in the Shadow of the Visionary, your vision is expanding out of control, so take the time you need to get grounded. Reconnect to your greater purpose, and ask with real curiosity, "What is my next baby step?" Once you return to Earth, you can take action to fulfill your vision with integrity.

High-Value Gifts

- Innovation
- Improvisation
- Mental brilliance
- Visionary
- Enlightened perspective
- Problem-solving
- Sociable nature
- Humanitarianism
- Courage
- Optimism

Inspired Action Plan

"I tap into divine guidance, wisdom, and knowledge for a higher vision of greater good for the world. I stay committed to bring my vision to fruition."

Tapping In with Your Visionary

Consult with your Visionary by meditating and journaling on the following questions to activate your unique high-value gifts and talents.

- What are my Visionary's high-value gifts and talents?
- How can I use these high-value gifts and talents in my current work or the work I want to be doing?
- What is one inspired action I can take today to do that?

Coming Out of The Shadows

- What aspects of The Visionary's shadow energy are present in my life right now?
- How does this shadow energy affect my connection to and expression of my divine purpose?
- What is one inspired action I can take today to release this shadow energy?

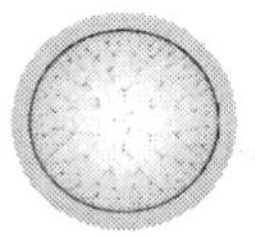

The Sage

(Jupiter)

WISE. SPIRITUAL. WEALTHY. GRACIOUS. INTUITIVE. INSPIRED. DEVOTED. EXPANSIVE. SELF-REFLECTIVE. TRUTH-SEEKING. EMOTIONALLY INTELLIGENT. TRUTHFUL. PHILOSOPHICAL. CHARITABLE. CONTEMPLATIVE.

MANTRA: "The truth will set me free."

SOUL DESIRE: To be a channel for truth and freedom.

PURPOSE: To use spiritual wisdom, knowledge, and intelligence to understand life and the world.

SHADOW: Righteous. Overconfident. Know-it-all.

The Sage is a wise, spiritual, and highly-intelligent guide who is connected to the deeper meaning in life and the world at large. The Sage can be known as an expert, advisor, scholar, counselor, professional, mentor, philosopher, researcher, healer, mystic, guru, or spiritual teacher.

As a Sage, you are in tune with the inner workings of the universe, and devoted to truth and freedom for all. Being a gracious soul, you desire the same freedom, truth, and wealth that you want for yourself for everyone else in the world.

You are gifted with a brilliant consciousness, and see the big picture and abundant possibilities for yourself, others, and the world. You are dedicated to positive change and growth, both internally and externally. You have the unique gift of making large concepts easily understandable by grounding them in relatable principles and proven strategies that others can easily assimilate and make practical use of in their lives.

You are an eternal student of higher knowledge, and believe that "to know is to grow." Wisdom is knowledge experienced. Others seek you out for both your knowledge and the wisdom in which you wrap that knowledge. Your superpower is helping others transcend life's challenges; by helping them understand the underlying lessons of their experiences, you help them to grow mentally, spiritually, and emotionally, and gain a greater sense of peace and freedom.

The Sage is social by nature, and possesses a generous spirit and compassionate heart. You can't help but uplift others with your sage advice—whether it's on the job, through social conversations, or with your loved ones. You are a highly-valued advisor who simplifies and clarifies complex situations so that businesses, projects, relationships, and lives can be propelled into motion.

The Shadow of The Sage

The know-it-all has forgotten the power of being an eternal student of higher knowledge. When you are in this shadow space, you limit possibilities because you are too absorbed by your own brilliance to see the bigger picture. Because you "already know," you limit your own access to the wisdom and knowledge you actually need to effectively solve the problem or mastermind the vision at hand. Plus, your arrogance can really piss people off.

Because you're expansive by nature, you can easily get attached to having more, doing more, and making more. You can become overconfident in your speculations, and overextend yourself and your resources (and even the resources of others). When you finally break, you will go down in flames, and others will lose trust in you.

If you find yourself in the shadow of The Sage, your ego is ruling your world. You've forgotten the true source of your knowledge and wisdom. It's time to reconnect with the deep well of your wisdom by giving yourself the solitude to meditate, contemplate, and commune with the pure source of truth and freedom. Read soul-stimulating texts, and invite even more expansive knowledge to find you and move through you to serve the world.

High-Value Gifts

- Wise teacher
- Has a huge vision
- Advisor
- Counsellor
- Mastermind
- Expert problem solver
- Simplifies large concepts

Inspired Action Plan

"I advance my high-value gift of wisdom by taking action on my knowledge to inspire and guide others to a deeper level of truth and freedom."

Tapping In with Your Sage

Consult with your Sage by meditating and journaling on the following questions to activate your unique high-value gifts and talents.

- What are my Sage's high-value gifts and talents?
- How can I use these high-value gifts and talents in my current work or the work I want to be doing?
- What is one inspired action I can take today to do that?

Coming Out of The Shadows

- What aspects of The Sage's shadow energy are present in my life right now?
- How does this shadow energy affect my connection to and expression of my divine purpose?
- What is one inspired action I can take today to release this shadow energy?

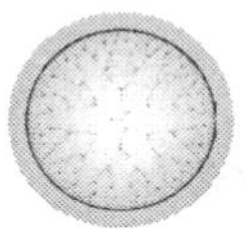

The Administrator

(Saturn)

PRACTICAL. GROUNDED. PERSEVERING. WISE. DEDICATED. STRONG. PURPOSEFUL. LEADING. ORGANIZED. STRUCTURED. CONFIDENT. STRATEGIC. ASSERTIVE. DISCIPLINED. HUMANISTIC. MORAL.

MANTRA: "I walk with a foot in both the earthly and spiritual worlds."

SOUL DESIRE: To be a grounded, social service-oriented leader who preserves and uplifts humanity.

PURPOSE: To responsibly lead and create practical systems and structures for the well-being of people, communities, and organizations.

SHADOW: Inner Critic. Over-Responsibility. Limited Viewpoint.

The Administrator is a grounded, persevering, service-oriented leader who is tapped into universal truth as a guiding principle. **The greatest purpose of the Administrator is to organize energy into its proper, practical form—the form which most positively serves humanity.**

As an Administrator, you are dedicated to establishing systems and structures that support the success and well-being of organizations and their people. You're often known as a leader, authority, teacher, controller, director, broker, agent, officer, executive, manager, spiritual leader, captain, supervisor, boss, or inspector.

Administrators expertly implement the prosperous hierarchy of progress and sustainability, and are therefore most at home running or managing a business, organization, project, or team. As an Administrator, you are not afraid to take risks—but you do prefer a calculated, consciously-designed approach to implementing big ideas. Patience and perseverance are two of your high-value gifts; they help you maintain equanimity so you can expertly regulate progress and quality of life for others.

You're a powerful leader and also can be an excellent entrepreneur who leads within a business or organization. You have the superpower of implementing process-based action, and are greatly respected for your innate ability to turn abstract concepts into practical action steps that others can follow to achieve what they want.

You have the currency of both earthly and spiritual wisdom, and confidently walk with a foot in both worlds. This gives you the detachment and objectivity you need to be of great service for all. You have a democratic approach, and put the needs of the many before the needs of the one. You're naturally disciplined in the true essence of the word; decibel of the One. You are valued for your reliability, systematic outlook, good boundaries, and longevity-based vision. You thrive when you have rhythm and routine in your work and personal life.

The Shadow of The Administrator

If judgment gets the best of you, your Inner Critic takes over. You may become attached to a perfect order or idea that exists nowhere near the realm of real possibility. Your Inner Critic may also tell you that, if you were worth your weight in salt, you should be able to make this 1000-foot-high jump. You end up harshly judging yourself, thinking that if anyone can do it, you should be able to. Failing to live up to your misguided standard is hell for you—and for everyone concerned with the situation. When you get into this pattern, you will spiral into negativity and self-torture as you desperately try to live up to the impossibly far-fetched standards of your Inner Critic. Needless to say, it's in your best interest—and the best interest of everyone around you—to avoid this scenario at all costs.

If you feel stressed because you've taken on too much work, then you can slip into over-responsibility. To avoid this, you must be clear about what you are truly responsible for, and stay in integrity with yourself. Otherwise, you will break down, wear out, get sick, or become depressed. Even the workhorse must remember to rest, or he will eventually end up limping and lame.

Everyone and everything has limits. If you are not in touch with yours, you will break down or fail. If you are stuck in a limiting viewpoint, you will find only obstacles and reasons why something can't happen, and may end up whining, complaining, and experiencing intense self-defeat. Instead, try to see the big picture, and all of the ways you can use your divine gifts to make it happen.

If you find yourself in the shadow of The Administrator, you have lost your footing in the spiritual world, and are firmly planted inside the limits of 3-D reality. It's time for a retreat, spiritual pilgrimage, or deep dive into a sacred text to quench your parched spiritual thirst and come home again to the balance of living in both worlds.

High-Value Gifts

- Natural leader
- Systematic
- Takes practical action
- Self-disciplined
- Highly responsible
- Establishes productive systems and structures
- Service-oriented
- Community-minded
- Considers the good of all
- Process-oriented
- Promotes sustainability
- Perseveres through adversity

Inspired Action Plan

"I practice the spiritual art of detachment to remain balanced in my high-value gifts, and lead those around me in establishing systems and structures that practically uplift humanity."

Tapping In with Your Administrator

Consult with your Administrator by meditating and journaling on the following questions to activate your unique high-value gifts and talents.

- What are my Administrator's high-value gifts and talents?
- How can I use these high-value gifts and talents in my current work or the work I want to be doing?
- What is one inspired action I can take today to do that?

Coming Out of The Shadows

- What aspects of The Administrator's shadow energy are present in my life right now?
- How does this shadow energy affect my connection to and expression of my divine purpose?
- What is one inspired action I can take today to release this shadow energy?

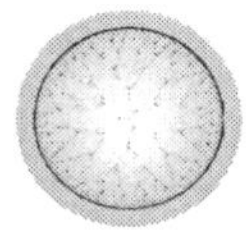

The Organizer

(Saturn)

PATIENT. PRACTICAL. TRUTHFUL. COMMITTED. STEADFAST. ORDERLY. RELIABLE. CONSIDERATE. CONSISTENT. DISCIPLINED. SYSTEMATIC. INSTINCTUAL. CAREFUL. DETAILED. DISCERNING. RATIONAL.

MANTRA: "Everything has its rightful place."

SOUL DESIRE: To be a channel for structuring energy and flow in practical form.

PURPOSE: To be aligned with divine order, and organize people, places, and things to support a higher quality of life.

SHADOW: Perfectionism. Stubbornness. Skepticism.

The Organizer is a practical, patient, reliable, and masterful steward who channels the energy of divine flow into practical form. **As an Organizer, you are attuned to the art of manifestation through proper placement, and innately know that putting things in their rightful place simplifies life and creates freedom.** You may be known as a coordinator, developer, arranger, facilitator, promoter, designer, consultant, instructor, coach, director, manager, or planner.

As an Organizer, you are intimately connected to the divine order which is at play in the universe. You have an eagle's eye for detail, and can connect resonant objects, people, and energies in ways that other people simply cannot. You have the high-value gift of assigning things their rightful place, especially in your chosen area of interest and expertise. Your superpower is sensing when something is missing; when it is, you can instinctually and immediately modify and restructure to promote the harmony and success of the whole.

You support people, businesses, and organizations in systematizing and grounding abstract ideas and concepts for practicality and profit. You're respected for your unique genius of composing and implementing process-based actions that support smooth operations and successful outcomes. You're a skilled problem solver with the exceptional ability to modify or restructure current systems to increase flow and make systems more user-friendly.

You have high standards and ideals, and are familiar with the fine line between great work and perfectionism. You expertly balance the process of creating the best solution with an imperative to bring a project to completion. Despite your high level of commitment to the task at hand, you practice detachment, and are humble enough to know that there are limits to what can be done with any set of conditions, resources, and time. As a result, you aim for simplicity, practicality, and longevity. When you hit your mark, you are thrilled to pieces—and when you have to compromise to get the job done, you surrender, make peace, and move on.

The Shadow of The Organizer

If you find yourself stuck in perfectionism, you have become too attached to your ideals and are stuck in the trap of "getting it right." You are being driven by your ego to be hyper-focused on an unattainable outcome. In the grip of this relentless contraction—which shows up as tightness in your jaw and gut—you can become seriously uptight, and squeeze the life right out of your project, your team, and yourself. When this happens, something is bound to break or break down; chances are, it will be you.

You know that "where there's a will, there's a way." However, when your will is not aligned with divine will, you will inevitably run into obstacles. More, you can become superlatively stubborn. This internal lockdown stops all forward momentum, and is frustrating not only for you, but for everyone you work with. When you are in a state of major resistance, you will not allow any new ideas or solutions to reach you; it's your way or the highway. No matter how brilliant you are, if you can't be flexible and solutions-oriented, no one will want to work with you.

It is good to look at things from all sides, and include possible failure scenarios in your calculations, but if you allow yourself to become too stressed or uptight you can become a major skeptic. Such a level of doubt will squeeze the life out of all possibilities, and render you unable to find the solutions you need. You'll remain stuck and unproductive until you shift your attitude.

If you find yourself in the shadow of The Organizer, chances are that you're overworked, too attached to outcomes, and cut off from your soul. It's time to put down "doing" and practice "being" so you can reconnect with divine order. You need to reconnect with Source and balance yourself through both meditation and a physical adventure like hiking, sailing, or traveling.

High-Value Gifts

- Dependable
- Trustworthy
- Perseverant
- Humble
- High standards
- Completes projects
- Simplifies systems, structures, and procedures
- Practical-minded
- Problem-solver
- Eye for detail
- Systematic
- Creates order out of chaos
- Turns abstract concepts into practical action

Inspired Action Plan

"I align with divine order and practice detachment so that I can utilize my high-value gifts to design systems and structures that support bringing the energy of flow into practical form for a higher quality of life."

Tapping In with Your Organizer

Consult with your Organizer by meditating and journaling on the following questions to activate your unique high-value gifts and talents.

- What are my Organizer's high-value gifts and talents?
- How can I use these high-value gifts and talents in my current work or the work I want to be doing?
- What is one inspired action I can take today to do that?

Coming Out of The Shadows

- What aspects of The Organizer's shadow energy are present in my life right now?
- How does this shadow energy affect my connection to and expression of my divine purpose?
- What is one inspired action I can take today to release this shadow energy?

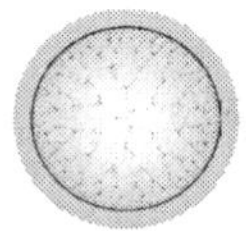

The Advocate

(Saturn)

HUMANITARIAN. RESOURCEFUL. INTEGROUS. IDEALISTIC. RESILIENT. OUTSPOKEN. OPINIONATED. REBELLIOUS. A CHAMPION. SUPPORTIVE. COMPASSIONATE. DEMOCRATIC. PASSIONATE. DRIVEN. DEVOTED.

MANTRA: "I align with the greater good for all."

SOUL DESIRE: To support and promote enduring positive social change.

PURPOSE: To be aligned with the Divine and present to the needs of the many in order to champion social change that uplifts humanity.

SHADOW: Self-serving behavior. Ignorance. Over-responsibility.

The Advocate is an outspoken, resourceful, devoted humanitarian whose soul motivation is to support positive social change. **As an Advocate, you are in touch with a higher possibility for mankind, and are on a mission to close the gap between the real needs of the everyday people in your field of expertise and the divine ideal for them.**

As an Advocate, you may be known as a humanitarian, ally, champion, promoter, consultant, defender, backer, supporter, sponsor, speaker, counselor, lawyer, journalist, blogger, or public relations expert. You have strong opinions, and are driven to champion the rights of others by improving organizations, institutions, communities, relationships, and social systems. You inspire and encourage people to give voice to what needs to be voiced in order to create positive change—even when that stance is unpopular. You are sensitive to what is amiss in social structures, and your "rebellious" streak serves your drive to create change—much like the irritant that develops the pearl. You don't let the important issues rest until justice has been accomplished.

Truth is your language, and you're willing to "fight the good fight" in its defense. You are also attuned to equality in people, and believe there is a place in your mission for anyone who desires to rise to the occasion. You're admired by others as a compassionate leader, and have a unique genius to activate empowerment in others and bind them together in action toward a greater calling. You are the first in the line of falling dominoes: you initiate the action that affects large-scale change.

You have the valuable currency of organization and initiation. You masterfully give form and order to whatever movement you currently serve, and help construct it to stand the test of time. You're a kind soul, and gifted with resilience; in the face of adversity, you gracefully pace yourself and your business or organization to persevere—and, ultimately, to triumph.

In your heart, you know that the balance between dedication to your cause and detachment from the outcome is the key to your overall success. You work best as your own boss, but are also highly valued by any organization fortunate enough to earn your affiliation.

The Shadow of The Advocate

You are powerful, and others look up to you as a leader who is aligned with the greater good. However, if you let your ego lead you away from the truth, you will end up placing your own needs and fulfillment above the needs of the many for whom you are supposed to be taking a stand. This will cause you to fall from grace. Without your platform to stand on, your world will contract with fear, and you will lose your direction, position, and purpose.

They say that ignorance is bliss. Not so for an Advocate. In your case, ignorance is believing that there are no limits to what you can do. If you become ungrounded or overconfident, you can overshoot what is possible, put too much at stake, and fall hard.

If you are stressed, you can become over-responsible when it comes to trying to eliminate others' suffering, and take on burdens that aren't yours to carry. You may also over-identify with what you do and accomplish, and believe that you are loved and valued only for those things. Remember that, although you are a valuable asset to your cause, business, or organization, you are not the only one who can handle a challenge or get the job done. You can be—and are—loved for being, not just doing.

High-Value Gifts

- Inspiring Leader
- Trustable
- Supports those in need
- Positive outlook
- Serves a greater cause
- Willing to take on difficult challenges
- Compassionate
- Speaks the truth
- Perseverant
- Organized
- Sensitive to the needs of the masses

Inspired Action Plan

"I align with the Divine to practice personal responsibility, and hone my high-value gifts to support and promote positive social change for the greater good of all."

Tapping In with Your Advocate

Consult with your Advocate by meditating and journaling on the following questions to activate your unique high-value gifts and talents.

- What are my Advocate's high-value gifts and talents?
- How can I use these high-value gifts and talents in my current work or the work I want to be doing?
- What is one inspired action I can take today to do that?

Coming Out of The Shadows

- What aspects of The Advocate's shadow energy are present in my life right now?
- How does this shadow energy affect my connection to and expression of my divine purpose?
- What is one inspired action I can take today to release this shadow energy?

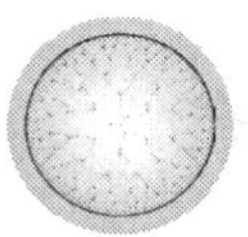

The Magician

(Rahu)

ACQUISITIVE. ALTERNATIVE. HIGHLY INTELLIGENT. CONSCIOUS. CREATIVE. UNIQUE. MAGICAL. INTUITIVE. INVENTIVE. ALCHEMIC. TECHNICAL. ARTISTIC. DYNAMIC. PSYCHOLOGICAL. SYNTHESIZING. ECCENTRIC. CHARISMATIC.

MANTRA: "I am a master manifestor."

SOUL DESIRE: To create freedom and make dreams come true.

PURPOSE: To be present and attuned to universal laws and use them to freely manifest on the earthly plane for the benefit of all.

SHADOW: Manipulative. Egocentric. Narcissistic. Paranoid. Overly materialistic. Greedy.

The Magician is a unique, highly-intelligent, ingenious manifestor whose fluency in both the laws of the universe and the laws of science makes it possible to create, acquire, and make things happen in the world.

As a Magician, you're a dynamic master transformer who walks to the beat of your own drummer. With equal footing in both the seen and unseen worlds, transformation and manifestation are your brands of magic. You may be known as an artisan, alchemist, inventor, healer, catalyst, visionary, actor, expert, genius, researcher, consultant, specialist, technician, scientist, psychologist, medicine woman, or shaman. Whatever your field of focus, you expertly transform situations, influence others, and manifest your vision on the earthly plane for the benefit of humanity.

You're nontraditional by nature, and the usual social and business categories cannot define you. Being innately tapped into the universal secrets of nature, the cosmos, and the soul gives you an extraordinary scope of knowledge and an evolutionary perspective. You thrive on playing at the edges of what's "possible," and aim to transcend time and space as you materialize your vision outside of the ordinary. This also means that you often rock the boat, disrupt the status quo, and agitate situations in an effort to force the essential truths to rise to the top. When you do this, you can alchemically unite only the purest elements of your project with new ideas and energies to create something entirely new.

The underlying gift of your work is that, in the process of transforming everything around you, you also undergo profound personal transformation. Your Magician's path is riddled with twists and turns, all of which bring great lessons to you and those you serve. "Mind over matter" is your motto; your mind is like a supercomputer, quickly synthesizing information and slicing through the chaos to the truth that transforms.

As a Magician, you are spirited, charismatic, and influential. You often dazzle others with your grand visions and endeavors, which you seem to magically accomplish from the inside out. Your superpowers of evolved consciousness and objectivity make you a trusted advisor.

You are clever, whip-smart, technical, and self-preserving, and possess a fearlessness that others admire. You're wired to be seen in the world, but are also astutely aware that fame and recognition come with a price. You choose your opportunities wisely, and make it a priority to stay connected to divine wisdom as you transform, manifest, and acquire in the material world.

The Shadow of The Magician

You're brilliant and masterful in your ability to wield the power of the universe for your desires. However, when you are using your knowledge solely for personal gain, your ego is taking over, and you can be tempted to manipulate and seize power over others.

If you find yourself manipulating those around you, you've slipped over to the dark side, and are dangerously cut off from the Divine. Manipulation is a seductive energy, and can show up very subtly as well as overtly; because you are such a powerful creator, this energy must be nipped in the bud to avoid causing irreparable harm. Eventually, you will get caught in your own tangled web, and create a lot of destruction for yourself and others.

If stressed, you can become hyper-focused, lose your balance, and become overly enamored with things like emotions, substances, or people. Your ability to intensely focus can serve you well, but you can have too much of a good thing. If you're intoxicated, you are seriously attached, which goes against universal law and leads to complication and drama. A glass or two of wine is fine—but if you keep drinking, get in your car, and end up in a ditch, drama and suffering will be waiting right around the corner.

You are wired to be a master manifestor, and your true path is to walk with one foot in the spiritual plane and one in the earthly plane. If you put too much focus on what you are manifesting, you will lose touch with the spiritual plane and become too materialistic. Greed is a high price to pay for your power: it will separate you from the Divine, burn important bridges, and distance you from those you love. You can buck every earthly system in pursuit of your magic, but when you start shrugging off the divine laws by which you create, you will feel the consequences. Remember, you always have a choice.

If you find yourself in the shadow of The Magician's energy, you are disconnected from the source of your being and your true power. It's high time you pull back from what you are creating, get back to your roots, and connect with a higher vision. Put everything on pause to engage in sacred ritual, go on a vision quest, or book a retreat to re-vision the most aligned path and purpose for your power.

High-Value Gifts

- Transformer
- Alchemist
- Innovator
- Technical ability
- Great researcher
- Brings new forms into being
- Creative Synthesizer
- Highly-skilled manifestor
- Artistic problem solver
- Solution oriented
- Out-of-the-box thinker
- Tapped into universal consciousness

Inspired Action Plan

"I stay attuned to a higher vision, and use my high-value gifts to help create freedom and make dreams come true for myself and others."

Tapping In with Your Magician

Consult with your Magician by meditating and journaling on the following questions to activate your unique high-value gifts and talents.

- What are my Magician's high-value gifts and talents?
- How can I use these high-value gifts and talents in my current work or the work I want to be doing?
- What is one inspired action I can take today to do that?

Coming Out of The Shadows

- What aspects of The Magician's shadow energy are present in my life right now?
- How does this shadow energy affect my connection to and expression of my divine purpose?
- What is one inspired action I can take today to release this shadow energy?

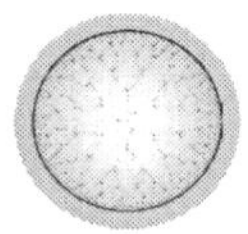

The Mystic

(Ketu)

SPIRITUAL. SENSITIVE. UNCONVENTIONAL. PERCEPTIVE. TRANSCENDENT. INTUITIVE. INTROVERTED. ILLUMINATING. ARTISTIC. INGENIOUS. INTENSE. IMAGINATIVE. INNOVATIVE. RELINQUISHING. REVOLUTIONARY. REBELLIOUS. MYSTERIOUS.

MANTRA: "I am spiritually wealthy."

SOUL DESIRE: To be a channel for transcending the material world.

PURPOSE: To bridge the spiritual and material worlds to create true freedom for myself and humanity.

SHADOW: Isolation. Lack of Balance. Victimhood. Fantasy.

The Mystic is an unconventional, intuitive, and highly perceptive seeker who is acutely aware of embodying both the human and the Divine. **Dedicated to the path of enlightenment, the Mystic's primary purpose is to bridge the spiritual and material worlds, discover the "deeper meaning" in life, and experience true freedom.**

As a Mystic, you may be known as a healer, seeker, inventor, artisan, spiritual leader, yogi, monk, astrologer, consultant, advisor, environmentalist, activist, researcher, or renunciate. You're highly invested in spiritual wealth, and will let go of the material world to turn within and seek for spiritual treasure. In your quest for true freedom, transcendence is your soul's primary motivation; you're masterful at living from the inside out.

Life has taught you the value of detachment, and you walk lightly in the material world while remaining firmly rooted with the Divine. You know that it's only the ego that experiences letting go as loss; you have learned to trust that, when you're called to renounce in the material world, you will be repaid a thousand fold in the spiritual world.

You're highly valued for the depth of insight you bring to every situation. You're unconventional in your approach to life and business, and are known for your gift of innovation. You're a visionary by nature, given to otherworldly perspectives and fluent in the energetics that lay behind the workings of the world. You're masterful at transforming old forms to new, and bringing forth alternative solutions that others have not thought of.

You have a rebellious side, and can be a catalyst for social change. You're designed to bring issues to the forefront, revolutionize them, shift them, and elevate the situation beyond the status quo. With your intuitive genius, you expertly illuminate the emerging qualities, ideas, and opportunities that are hidden beneath the surface of an issue. You have an eagle's eye for detecting and unearthing toxicity, limiting beliefs, and patterns that are holding back people and organizations from integrity and truth.

The Shadow of The Mystic

You're an introvert, and need ample time alone to attend to your inner life. However, you must be careful not to isolate yourself from the world. If you're not actively engaged in your relationships and work, you will end up lonely and depressed.

You don't ever feel completely at home in this physical world. This detachment from the material is part of what gives you your transcendent viewpoint. If you are not firmly connected with the

Divine, though, this detachment will be lost, and you will slip into victimhood. Without your broader spiritual perspective, you will think your life is happening *to* you, rather than *for* you, and blame others for your circumstances.

You have a great imagination that allows you to entertain many possible realities. If you are ungrounded and not purposefully engaged in your life, you can end up stuck in your head with a distorted perception of life or spirituality. Living in this fantasy world may be fun for a while, but eventually you will have to deal with the harsh reality of loss and suffering that could have been avoided if you had been able to see clearly.

You are very sensitive, and if stressed, your focus can become too extreme in one domain. This can lead you to become seriously unbalanced. Much like an out-of-control race car, the other areas of your life will quickly crash and burn.

If you find yourself in the shadow of the Mystic's energy, you have become disconnected from the awareness that you are both human and divine. It is time to reconnect through your spiritual practice and reengage with your worldly purpose. Get your feet on the ground in nature, move your body, and embrace your like-minded and like-hearted community.

High-Value Gifts

- Innovative
- Intuitive
- Creative thinker
- Detached
- Great insight
- Transcends physical limitations
- Highly perceptive
- Strong "detective" abilities
- Breaks limiting patterns
- Connects the unlikely
- Creates new ways of doing things

Inspired Action Plan

"I am present to both my inner and outer life so I can hone my high-value gifts to bridge the spiritual and material world and create freedom for myself and humanity."

Tapping In with Your Mystic

Consult with your Mystic by meditating and journaling on the following questions to activate your unique high-value gifts and talents.

- What are my Mystic's high-value gifts and talents?
- How can I use these high-value gifts and talents in my current work or the work I want to be doing?
- What is one inspired action I can take today to do that?

Coming Out of The Shadows

- What aspects of The Mystic's shadow energy are present in my life right now?
- How does this shadow energy affect my connection to and expression of my divine purpose?
- What is one inspired action I can take today to release this shadow energy?

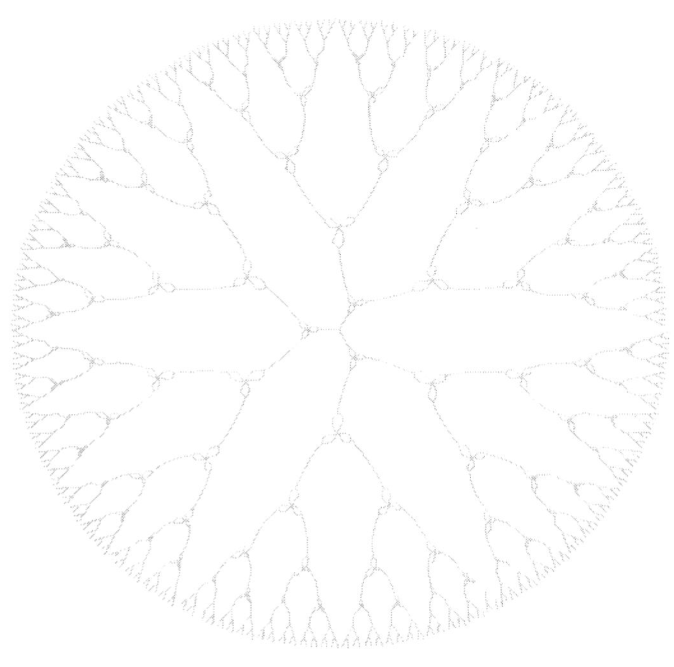

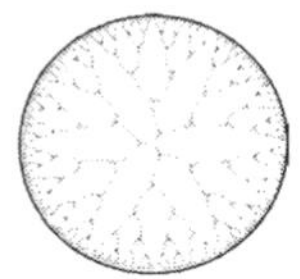

Chapter Eight

ACTIVATE YOUR ARCHETYPES

Now that you've chosen your Sacred Wealth Archetypes (or, more accurately, now that they have chosen you!) it's time to get to know them better, and learn what they have to teach you about your Sacred Wealth Code, your high-value gifts, and your path to prosperity.

The first time I truly found my Sacred Wealth Code and met my Wealth Council in the form of my Archetypes, it felt magical, like a sacred homecoming. I know the same will be true for you. The more you tune in with your Sacred Wealth Archetypes and take inspired action on what they teach you, the more at home you will be at your personal intersection of purpose and prosperity.

This process will stretch and grow you, of course—but like all soul challenges, it is for your highest good. There are gifts beyond your imagination waiting for you on the other side.

Your Archetypes are the best of you. As you get to know them, you will also be learning about the highest aspects of yourself. Be willing, as we move forward together in this process, to notice how you've already been using your gifts, where you have been denying your gifts, and where you can infuse a bigger dose of your superpowers. Be willing to learn what you need to know to be brilliant in your own unique, soul-driven way.

Remember, we all support each other when we use our high-value gifts. Also remember that your high-value gifts—the gifts about which your Archetypes are going to teach you—are what people really want to pay you for. Your Archetypes are the golden keys to the house of your gifts which is located at the intersection of purpose and prosperity. The more you tune in with your Sacred Wealth Archetypes, the more secrets they will show you about the place your soul feels most at home.

DEVELOP A RELATIONSHIP WITH YOUR ARCHETYPES

How did it feel to meet your Archetypes? Were there some surprises there for you? Did you recognize gifts and talents you already knew about, or did you discover something new about yourself and your own potential?

Whatever your initial experience, the best way to continue to develop and deepen your relationship with your Archetypes is to engage with them as often as possible. Reading their descriptions daily, working with the "Tapping In" questions at the end of each description, and meditating on the archetypal energies will inform you greatly. Even if you only spend a few minutes each day doing this, you will begin to notice a shift almost immediately.

As you sit each day with your Archetypes, ask for them to show themselves to you in your daily life. Ask to see where their energies are already present in your work, your passion, and your purpose.

More, ask that all-important question we've been working with since the beginning of this book: "What is one inspired action I can take today?" Ask your Archetypes for inspired actions to perform, and then execute those actions. When you do this, you will not only begin to relate more strongly to your Archetypes, you will begin to trust them, and see how what they offer is directly connected to your wealth and prosperity.

Once you get comfortable with your Archetypes, you can also ask them for specific help and advice. You can tap into their energy for information about how to proceed with a specific event, a certain part of your business … anything at all that you're creating. You can also ask for information about which of your high-value gifts would be most useful to bring to this project. Listen to what your Archetypes and your soul have to tell you, and then take whatever inspired actions are revealed.

Again, your Sacred Wealth Archetypes are your Wealth Council. They are your feedback team, your coaches, your internal mastermind group. Once you learn how to listen skillfully, they will share with you everything you need to know about how to live on purpose and create wealth in a way that is totally aligned with your unique Sacred Wealth Code. Soon, you will embody their energies so seamlessly that you'll hardly need to think about it.

So don't hold back. Tap into these energies. Invite them into your life. Listen to what they have to say with your whole body, mind, and heart. Then, take inspired action, and watch the opportunities flow.

THE SHADOW SIDES OF YOUR ARCHETYPES

If you connected more to the shadow sides of some of your Archetypes than to their light aspects, there's no reason to panic, or judge yourself. In fact, as we learned in Chapter Seven, the pathways to our greatest superpowers often lead us through our greatest challenges.

The shadow side of an Archetype is what manifests when the energy of that Archetype is no longer tapped into the grounding, loving, positive energy of your soul, and is instead operating from the ungrounded, reactionary energy of your human ego, cultural programming, and subconscious belief systems. It's what happens when you leave your soul's neighborhood and the home of your high-value gifts and drag your Archetype with you on a misguided road trip.

Let's face it: we all have challenges that try to keep us from our brilliance, hold us back, and keep us circling the neighborhood of our Sacred Wealth Code without ever turning down our home street. We all get scared sometimes, and react out of that fear instead of from a place of certainty in our own power. But these challenges are temporary. They can only keep us lost and stuck if we refuse to learn from them.

That's why it's vital for you to embrace the shadow aspects of your Archetypes as well as the light. When you are willing to include and embrace even the shadowy parts of yourself, you can work with them. You can bring them into the light. But if you're shutting a part of yourself out of the room, you will never get to know it. You won't find out what its real motivations are, or how to bring them into the light in a positive way.

As Carl Jung taught: "What you resist, persists."

If you are living in the shadow of one or more of your Archetypes, you are only a shift away from embodying their superpowers. As with any relationship, it's all about learning to have the right conversations. With practice, you'll learn to recognize when you are slipping into that shadow energy, and correct your course before you veer away from your Sacred Wealth Code.

In most cases, you can connect with your shadow and resolve it by looking at your beliefs. Usually, it is a belief, not an outside circumstance, that's driving you into the shadow energy. Once you unplug from that negative belief and into the power source of your Sacred Wealth Code and high-value gifts, you can shift your relationship to the shadow so that it no longer feels like it's controlling you.

Wealth Alignment Practice 8

As you've become accustomed to doing, take a few deep breaths to tune in and bring your mind down into your heart. Feel your soul. Tune in to what it's saying to you.

Next, bring into your awareness the challenge that you're currently having, or the shadow energy that you're embodying. **Ask yourself: "What is the belief that's driving this energy?"** Ask this question several times with an open mind and heart until that hidden belief reveals itself.

When that belief reveals itself, don't go back into your head. Don't judge it, or push it away. Instead, draw it closer. Hold it with compassion.

Maybe you're avoiding your superpowers because you believe you're not good enough to use them wisely. Maybe you're hiding in the shadow of your Archetype because you're afraid to be seen for who you really are. Maybe you believe that there's not enough wealth to go around, and that you have to fight for yours instead of simply inviting it.

Whatever your belief is, write it down. As you do, envision yourself embracing this belief like you would a frightened child. Hold it close to your heart, and comfort it. Your soul knows that these fears are real to *you*, but that they are not real.

Now that you've calmed your fear, really look at it. Gaze into its eyes. More, see where you're plugged into the story it's been telling you. You might visualize it as a cable or cord, with one end plugged into your heart and the other end into your fear.

Next, ask your soul, "Which of my Archetypes embodies the opposite of my fear?" What is the other end of the spectrum from what you're experiencing? If you're afraid of judgment, which Archetype embodies self-certainty? If you're afraid of being unworthy, which Archetype embodies worth? And if you're afraid of scarcity, which Archetype most embodies easeful abundance? Invite that part of your Wealth Code to enter the space you've created, and ask it to help you unplug from your fear, and the story it's told you, with love and compassion.

Finally, take the loose end of that cord and plug it into the essence of your Archetype. Take a deep breath and feel the rush of new energy flood into your being. Feel the new ease in your heart and mind. Feel how empowering it is to stand in the light instead of hiding in the shadow.

However the above exercise plays out for you—whether you actually "see" these events happening or simply feel them—trust what you're experiencing. You are redirecting energy away from your challenges and into your empowerment.

Once you feel fully connected to your new power source, ask yourself, "What is one inspired action I can take today to support myself in living into this new empowerment?" Then, put that action on your calendar, and do it. Once you do, you'll start to feel a difference almost immediately.

Here's what such a shift can look like in practice:

Tracy was getting aligned with her Sacred Wealth Code, and things were really starting to flow for her both creatively and financially. She had a business where she helped people communicate more constructively and create better relationships. But the more she dug in and got to know her Archetypes, the more she realized that she was still, in some ways, cutting herself off. She wasn't completely trusting herself or her intuition. She constantly felt the need to evaluate and explain where her knowledge came from, instead of simply flowing with it or dismissing it.

As we dug into the belief behind that separation, we found that she had an old belief that told her that her intuition wasn't valuable. And so, she used her superpower of intuition only privately, instead of bringing it out into its full power and potential. The trouble was, in the work she was doing, she needed her intuition more than ever before.

Together, we performed the exercise I've described above, and unplugged her from that old belief. Then, we redirected her energy toward the light aspects of her Archetypes and gifts, so that they were filling her up instead of disempowering her. Once she was able to fully embody her Connector, she was able to trust herself, connect more deeply with those she was serving, find the fulfillment she'd been missing, and take her business to the next level.

If you find yourself up against the shadow side of your Archetypes, give yourself time to work with your fears and ingrained beliefs. It's natural to backslide a little bit at first. After all, you're leaving familiar territory and heading into the unknown. But these wrong turns won't hold you back unless you let them. They're simply reminders to tune in, pay attention to what you need to clear, and take inspired action.

As you continue to check in with the light aspects of your Archetypes on a regular basis, check in with the shadow aspects as well. Notice if you are feeling or behaving in a way that is leading down a ramp to shadow. If you do, again, don't judge. Instead, stop what you're doing, check in with your soul, and ask for a new set of directions. Each time you do this, you'll be able to step back into your power more quickly and easily.

You are creating transformation that can last a lifetime. You're bringing the highest aspects of your soul energy and your Sacred Wealth Code down into your body—and sometimes, the results may feel a bit alien at first. So be patient, loving, and kind to yourself, and remember that each step you take will bring you closer to living from your Sacred Wealth Code.

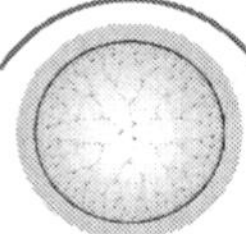

Wealth Focus

More Ways to Connect with Your Archetypes

1 Choose one of your Archetypes to focus on. Then, choose one of your high-value gifts that relates to that Archetype, and focus on putting that gift into action today. In how many ways can you use that gift? How does it connect you with your wealth dream? Do this over multiple days with multiple gifts, and see what happens!

2 To embody the energy of one of your Archetypes, try wearing something that reminds you of your Archetype—such as a specific color, piece of jewelry, or perfume.

3 Pick someone you know (or someone famous or historical) who reminds you of your Archetype or gifts. Read about them, get a picture of them, or choose a quote from them, and post it in your workspace.

4 Create a vision board or collage that reminds you of one of your Archetype's high-value gifts. Focus on how your life will look when you are fully embodying that Archetype and its gifts.

5 Light a candle and meditate on the energy of your Archetype for a minute or two. Then, blow the candle out.

6 Listen or dance to music that evokes the energy of your Archetype and makes you feel empowered with your gifts.

7 Write down your Archetype's "inspired action plan" statement from its description in this book, or create your own. Post this statement where you will see it often.

8 Choose the cards which represent your Archetypes from the Sacred Wealth Code Oracle Deck* and keep them where you can see them and read them at least once a day—on your desk, on your refrigerator, or on your car's dashboard.

*Available at www.SacredWealthCode.com

Reflection

Journal about or meditate on the following statement:

"If I tell myself the truth …"

How did I know that the Archetypes I connected with in this chapter were part of my Wealth Council? What does that knowing teach me about how to communicate with my soul?

______

______

______

______

How do I feel about the Archetypes I identified as part of my Wealth Council? Have I placed any judgments on them—and, if so, how can I embrace them more fully?

______

______

______

______

______

Were there any Archetypes I wished were mine, but weren't?

How have I embodied the energy of my Archetypes recently?

What have I learned by delving into the shadow energy of my Archetypes?

Action Step

Repeat the exercises for connecting with your Archetypes and unplugging from shadow energy from earlier in this chapter.

In particular, work with the questions, "What do my Archetypes have to teach me today?" and "What is one inspired action I can take today to embody my Archetype(s)?" Be sure to follow through on any instructions you receive.

Write your notes in the space below.

Part IV

SACRED WEALTH INTEGRATION

The Integration Process

Congratulations! You've tapped into the Four Pillars of your Sacred Wealth Code, and identified the Archetypes which embody the energies of your high-value gifts, passions, and soul challenges. You have taken a deep dive into your own truth, and come out with a greater understanding of who you are, what you want, and where you want to go.

Simply knowing all of this isn't enough, however. Knowledge alone doesn't create transformation. In order to put your Sacred Wealth Code to work in your life, you have to translate that knowledge into action.

It's time to take everything you've learned in this book and put it all together, so you can take inspired action every day, wield your superpowers with ease, expand your gifts, create your wealth dream, and live on purpose in ways you've never before imagined.

As you continue to live in harmony with your Wealth Code, your gifts, talents, and Archetypes will continue to reveal more and more of themselves. They will not only bring you prosperity: they will bring you joy, and the deep sense of fulfillment that is part of real wealth.

Your feet will be planted, firmly and flexibly, on your true wealth path—the path where you're creating wealth by doing what you love.

You will achieve soul goals and milestones, and set new ones that you may never have imagined were possible. Your intentions will no longer be simply intentions; they will actually manifest, and in bigger and brighter ways than you can imagine.

Things in all areas of your life will get easier. You will have more grace and flow. Even things that take a lot of energy will feel easier because you're inspired and aligned, and using your superpowers.

Your confidence will increase greatly, because you will know that you are doing what you have always been called to do. You can live into your vision of wealth because the best of you is activated and present in your everyday life.

You will have clarity. Clarity is power. When you're clear, you trust more. You enjoy more. You're happier. You have more time for the things in life that you really want to be doing. And, most of all, you take soul-directed, inspired action without question or hesitation.

You will know that there is always a way, and that your Sacred Wealth Code will help you discover that way. You will know that the universe is on your side, taking care of you.

You will feel a deep sense of satisfaction, because you will know that you are doing what you came here to do. You know that you can give up on striving, because your true path—the path toward your soul—will nourish you along the way. Your fulfillment and satisfaction ooze out of you; they're contagious, and they uplift others.

You will make more money. You will have more flow of abundance and wealth coming directly from what you're doing—and also from places you never thought or imagined, because the universe is conspiring for you to receive everything you need to fulfill your purpose. You will attract exactly the right people and opportunities into your world, at exactly the right times. You will receive promotions in your career or business, because you're seen and valued for your unique superpowers.

Alignment from the inside out creates congruency in everything. Because you're aligned with your soul, your purpose, and your superpowers, other areas of your life will also fall into place. Relationships, parenting, creative endeavors … all will flourish.

All of this is possible for you. It's right around the corner. But in order to experience the magic and promise of your Sacred Wealth Code, you must make it an integral part of your life, and engage with it from your soul outward, in every part of your life. You need to move beyond knowing and visioning, and into daily inspired action and interaction. You need to get intimate with your soul-given superpowers and use them as often as possible, so you can own your brilliance all the way down to the soles of your feet.

Your Sacred Wealth Code is your vehicle. Your Four Pillars are your destination, and your Archetypes are your guides. You now have everything you need to drive to your wealth dream.

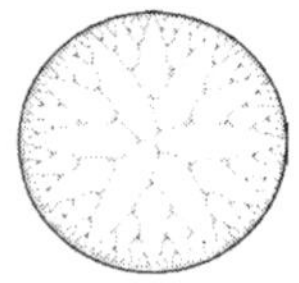

Chapter Nine

WORKING WITH YOUR SACRED WEALTH CODE

As you invite your Sacred Wealth Code into your daily life, you will grow into your gifts—and, in turn, your gifts will grow you.

By tapping in regularly with your Four Pillars, your Archetypes, and your soul's wisdom, you are developing a relationship with the best of yourself. Over time, you will learn to trust yourself, and the guidance you receive from your Wealth Code, deeply and fully. It might feel like you're stretching to begin with (especially if your high-value gifts are a bit rusty, or you have some unhelpful beliefs to work through around your superpowers) but this discomfort is only temporary. The more you dive into it, the faster it will resolve.

When you listen deeply, and take inspired action based on the information you receive, the Divine will speed your feet in the right direction—your wealth direction. You will see the results of using your high-value gifts in real time as wealth shows up in your life. You will see change within yourself, within the work that you're doing, within the people with whom you associate. This change will compound and escalate the more you engage with your Wealth Code.

For this to happen, you need to do this work continually, not just once or twice. You need to establish an intimate, long-term relationship with your soul, your Four Pillars, your superpowers, and your Archetypes.

If you really want to create wealth in a way that's on purpose and aligned with your soul, you can't afford *not* to do this.

GROWING INTO YOUR GIFTS

When Tara received her Sacred Wealth Code, she really took it to heart. She tuned in with at least one of her Archetypes every day, and consistently walked away from her practice with one piece of information about her high-value gifts that really stood out to her. She would then put that information into practice that day, through inspired action, and note the results.

If she had anything going on with the shadow of that day's Archetype, she would also ask for an inspired action to move past that shadow, or a practice to clear that energy.

She had always loved being a creative and a teacher, and those gifts and talents opened up even more for her once she engaged with her Sacred Wealth Code. However, it was when she also embraced her Organizer and Leader Archetypes, and cleared the shadow energies that were keeping her from fully embodying her superpowers in those areas, that everything started to fall into place in her life and business.

In a relatively short period of time, Tara found that she didn't have to *think* about the work so much anymore. She didn't have to ask herself who her Archetypes were, because she was embodying them. Her Wealth Council was with her, always, and often spoke through her as she taught and coached others to open up to their creativity. More, she was prolifically creating powerful new content, and easily attracting new clients and opportunities.

All of this took several months to evolve. But it would never have happened without Tara's willingness to practice being in her Sacred Wealth Code, every day, without fail. That consistency made her Wealth Code an instinctive part of her, instead of a foreign language which took effort to understand.

Here's another example of a Wealth Code at work.

Right after Theresa aligned with her Sacred Wealth Code, she was heading to the airport from her friend's house, where she'd been visiting. When she got there, the flight was full, but the desk person offered her an opportunity to take a less-full flight the next day and receive an $800 voucher with the airline for a future flight.

Of course, Theresa was thrilled. Her friend's house was only five minutes from the airport, and she was able to not only spend another night with her friend, but also have airfare for two more trips she was planning. Driving back to her friend's place, she realized that she had just made $800 *without doing anything.*

Since that day, Theresa has also received a promotion in her teaching career, attracted more clients to her private practice, and experienced multiple synchronicities where money lands unexpectedly in her lap. She attributes all of this to fully aligning with her Sacred Wealth Code. Her Muse is always talking to her, she says, keeping her awareness on the places where divine abundance is waiting for her.

If you want to experience the kinds of synchronicity and ease that Tara and Theresa did, you will want to align with your gifts every day, and take the inspired actions that are revealed to you.

Use the Wealth Focus exercises on the next several pages to craft your daily practice.

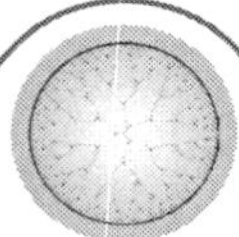

Wealth Focus

Connect with Your High-Value Gifts Every Day

1 Get out and try new things—especially things that support you in using your high-value gifts. Take a class. Join a like-hearted cause or community. Volunteer, or start a project. Whatever puts your gifts into play and makes you feel good, do it.

2 Express appreciation for your gifts. Choose one gift per day to work with. Write it down, then ask yourself, "Why (or how) does this gift make my life more wonderful?" Then, write down everything that comes to mind, and read your answers to yourself throughout the day.

3 At the end of each day, before bed, reflect on your day. How did you put your high-value gifts to work? Where did you have opportunities to use your gifts, but didn't? Create an action plan to use your gifts even more prolifically in the coming days.

4 Journal about one (or more) of your gifts every day, and all the ways you can use your superpowers in your business, projects, or life. Get creative, and let your imagination run free. Then, take inspired action on one idea per day.

5 Watch for scenes where your gifts play out—not only in your own life, but in movies, on TV, in books, in business, and anywhere else you observe people regularly. Become aware of how others use their high-value gifts, and how you can use your own.

Inspired Action Plan

Create a 30-day action plan for engaging with the Four Pillars of your Wealth Code and one or more of your Archetypes on a daily basis.

1 Write out your wealth vision, purpose, passion, superpowers, greatest challenges, and Archetypes, and keep them in a place where you can see and read them often.

2 Go back through the exercise and Wealth Focus questions in this book, as well as your own notes. If both are reflective of where you are now, use these as the basis for your plan. If not, do all of the exercises again so your information is aligned with who and where you are today.

3 Make a list of exercises, meditations, and action steps that suit your personal style and help you feel connected. These will be the basis of your daily action plan.

4. Revisit the exercises in this chapter, as well as those in Chapter Eight, to create a daily action plan for engaging with your Four Pillars and your Archetypes. You might choose a different approach each day, or create a consistent daily practice; either one is fine as long as you are tuning in with your Sacred Wealth Code and Wealth Council every day, asking for inspired actions, and taking them.

5. No matter what, get your Sacred Wealth Code discovery time on your calendar right away. Don't schedule so much time that it feels like a burden, but stretch yourself enough to get out of your comfort zone and habitual modes of operation.

6. Stick to your plan for at least 30 days, and take note of what you discover. After 30 days, you can tweak your plan to include any new information you've received.

7. If you have a friend who is also on a Sacred Wealth Code journey, set up an accountability system and check in with one another about your progress, gratitudes, successes, and challenges.

THE PRUNING PROCESS

The process of aligning with your Sacred Wealth Code and your Archetypes is more than merely an exercise. You are shifting into a new way of being.

At times, this can mean that things which are not aligned with your Wealth Code will simply fall away. These things can include major parts of your life—like an old job, an old business, or old relationships. However, it's important to remember that, just as pruning a tree causes it to grow in a healthier and more directed way, this "pruning" of your life is for your greatest good. And, if you tell yourself the truth, you will realize that you already knew at some level that the things which are falling away from your life were not in full alignment with your wealth, your purpose, your passion, your gifts, or your Archetypes.

If changes (big or small) come to you as a result of your work with your Wealth Code, don't fight them—but don't force them, either. Getting impatient or frustrated will only steer you away from the place you are headed—your soul's neighborhood, and the intersection of your purpose and prosperity. Be willing to dive into the uncertainty, and let things flow. Remember that the universe and the Divine are pruning you so that you can bloom more beautifully.

Remember, aligning with your Wealth Code isn't just about money. It's about living a wealthy life—a life that provides everything you need to fully express your purpose, passion, and superpowers.

Just like any superhero, you will also have challenges. Your pruning process may include some of your soul challenges, working through the shadow side of one or more of your Archetypes, or clearing out old habits and mindsets that were creating obstacles around your high-value gifts. This process, as we explored in Chapter Eight, is a perfect way to practice using your superpowers. So be patient. Remember that there is something in this for you, as long as you keep up your daily practice, and invite your Sacred Wealth Code to guide you through whatever emerges. At the end of this pruning process, you will feel like doors have opened into a greater vision of *you*.

If you find yourself in the pruning process, try the following:

- Start a gratitude journal. Every day, list five things that you appreciate about yourself, your Sacred Wealth Code, your gifts, or the new directions your life is going.
- Find supporters. Surround yourself with people who appreciate your gifts.
- Take the high road. When faced with change, especially when it feels like you are losing someone or something, take the high road. Don't fight it. Just surrender, and let go gracefully. You are making space for relationships or opportunities that are aligned with the best of you.
- Repeat this simple prayer whenever letting go is challenging: "I bless you and release you in peace." (Or, "I bless this and release this in peace.")

Living a soul-aligned life is a full-contact sport. You need to be all-in to win. When you fall down, you need to get up as quickly as you can, and get back in the game. Even a full-out body tackle isn't cause to give up for the whole season. This pruning process is temporary, and you *will* grow from it, as long as you're willing to stand up, dust yourself off, and give it another try.

How To Know When You're Not Aligned with Your Sacred Wealth Code

If you become lax about engaging with your Archetypes and your Four Pillars, you may find yourself slipping out of alignment with your Wealth Code. It's okay. It happens. But when it does, you will want to take steps to correct it as soon as possible.

You will know that you are out of alignment because you'll be frustrated and overwhelmed. Quite simply, things will get hard.

This won't feel the same as going through your soul challenges or growing your gifts. It will be more like trying to wade through a swamp without a compass. You'll feel tension, anxiety, and contraction. The wealth, love, and opportunities you're trying to create will not flow. Your time may be eaten up with things you don't want to be doing. Struggle, conflict, and unnecessary drama will abound, and clients and customers may fall away for no obvious reason. Life doesn't have the joy, meaning, and ease you wish it did.

If any of this is happening for you, you have slipped out of alignment with your Sacred Wealth Code. It's time to step back and get reconnected with each of your Four Pillars, your Archetypes, and the heart of your wealth dream. Where are you ignoring or failing to use your high-value gifts? Where can you embody the positive aspects of your Archetypes? Where are you refusing to connect with your soul and the messages it's speaking to you?

Daily reconnection is the remedy for what you're going through. If necessary, start working with this book again at Chapter One, and go through the process of re-identifying all aspects of your Wealth Code from scratch. You may receive even more clarity in this second round, and see new pathways to your soul's neighborhood.

Above all, don't give up! You are doing this work for a great reason: your own purpose, prosperity, and highest good. You have the potential to live beyond your current capacities. You only need to choose that path, and take the inspired actions necessary to move forward.

Your Wealth Code is part of you—it's written into your soul blueprint. Even if you lose sight of it for a little while, it doesn't disappear. So, when things look bleak, don't give up. Something even more magnificent is waiting for you on the other side of this darkness.

THE PATH FORWARD

You now have everything you require to access, live from, and create from your Sacred Wealth Code!

Life as you know it will change from this point forward—and the more you work with your Four Pillars, your superpowers, and your Archetypes, the more rapid and sweeping that change will be.

Embrace this part of your journey! You are on the path of your wealth dream, heading home to the neighborhood of your soul.

Afterword

Thank you for engaging wholeheartedly with this body of work. By now you understand how to uncover, align with, and act through your Sacred Wealth Code in a way that manifests your greatest wealth dreams and your unique vision for your life.

You have always known these parts of yourself: your purpose, your passion, your gifts and challenges, and the energies of your Archetypes. Now, they are fully in your consciousness, and it's up to you how you choose to include them in your daily life.

Like anything else, working with your Sacred Wealth Code takes practice. However, because of the nature of this work, this is a fun, enlightening, and interesting practice that bears fruit each and every time you engage with it. Some elements will feel natural to you from the outset; others will feel new and strange, but the more you dive in, the easier these aspects will become.

You can keep your Sacred Wealth Code alive and active in your daily life by being willing to bring your Four Pillars and your Archetypes into everything you do: your projects, your current career, and your creative ventures. Make this work a natural part of your daily life.

Even if you notice yourself slipping into the shadow energy of your Archetypes, don't stop engaging with them. There are always great gifts in store for you when you bring your fears, hesitations, and unhelpful habits into the light. After all, fear is just love moving in the wrong direction.

I hold the vision of a world where every one of us is living on purpose, using our high-value gifts, and gifting each other and the world with our purpose, passion, and talents. When each of us are leading in our own way, and making a difference, we will also be aligned with the best of ourselves, and inviting wealth not only for ourselves, but for the world.

When you step into that greater vision, tap into your divine gifts, live on purpose, and use your high-value gifts, you will not only invite a massive shift toward your own wealth, prosperity, success, and happiness, you will be inviting others in your world to follow your example.

It's all within your grasp. It's the promise of your Sacred Wealth Code. All you have to do is take daily inspired action, stay aligned with your Four Pillars and the energy of your Archetypes, and watch the magic unfold.

May you live, from this moment forward, in wealth, prosperity, purpose, passion, and joy.

With love,
Prema

Acknowledgments

I am deeply honored, humbled, and grateful for being blessed with so much love and support by all the beautiful people who helped me birth this book. You call me to open my heart wider and step into my greatness. I love you all dearly.

Love and gratitude to my dear friend Dr. Kimberly McGeorge for seeing my gifts, holding my feet to the fire, and reminding me that it was time to write this book, and for always being there to help me to stay on my true path.

Heartfelt gratitude to soul sisters Margaret Saizan and Rebecca Loveless for your love and devotion, brilliant feedback to keep me on point, and generously holding space for me in my process. I am eternally grateful.

I am grateful to all my teachers along my journey and especially grateful to my brilliant Vedic Astrology mentor, Dennis Flaherty, for inviting me to study this science of light, claim my place as a Jyotish, and artfully use Vedic Astrology to uplift others.

Waves of gratitude for all the beautiful souls throughout the years who have shown up as my clients and students. Your desire to know your purpose, be more authentic, and create prosperity on your own terms has opened the door for this body of work to come through me.

Immense gratitude to my editor, Bryna René Haynes, for her expertise, steadfast support, brilliant wordsmithing, artistic design, and intuition, and for asking the really hard questions to keep this work pure and make sure that you, the reader, have everything you need to make the best possible use of this work. Creativity is a personal process, and needs trusted, loving support. Bryna, you have given me exactly what I've needed on this creative journey. Bless you.

Great appreciation for the love and support of my family. My dad, who believes in me, and taught me that there is always a way to figure things out. My sister, Kim, for her love, and for always cheering me on. My children Allegra and Colin, who always inspire me with their fresh perspectives, and who are two of my best teachers and best friends.

So much gratitude to my dearest Michael who generously gives me the love and support to stretch my wings and go for my dreams. He wants for me what I want for myself. For this, I am so very blessed.

About the Author

Prema Lee Gurreri is committed to creating a world where everyone is empowered to live on purpose, in a way that is aligned with their divine gifts and their birthright of true prosperity.

Prema guides and teaches entrepreneurs, visionaries, and change agents to lead with their unique, divine gifts and talents, and fully align with their purpose and passion to create wealth for themselves and the world simply by being who they are and doing what they love to do.

She believes that our core purpose is to be true to ourselves so we can claim our power and wholeness and manifest wealth in our own unique and meaningful ways. When we do what we are uniquely great at—rather than what we are merely good at—we invoke the power of our soul blueprint and our divine birthright. She created her Soulutionary® programs and services to empower clients to lead lives poised at the intersection of prosperity and purpose, and live from the hearts of their Sacred Wealth Codes.

Prema is a leading Vedic Astrologer, business consultant, energy practitioner, and spiritual coach with more than twenty-five years of experience. In her work, she draws from all of these life-changing practices and modalities to work with clients one-on-one and in group settings, in person and virtually. She also presents to groups as an inspired speaker, guide, and workshop facilitator.

There is work that you are meant to do in the world. There is work that you are meant to serve the world by doing. When you work with Prema, she closes the gap between inspiration and action by revealing your Soul Success Map™ and helping you unlock your Sacred Wealth Code® to discover your unique, divine gifts and talents. With these tools, you can quickly move your mission and business forward doing the work you are meant to do and experience a new level of prosperity, freedom, peace, and fulfillment.

Currently, Prema lives outside of Seattle, Washington with her beloved partner and their Standard Poodle, Bella. When she's not working, you can find her hanging out with her two grown children, digging in her garden, hiking along the beach, or star gazing.

Learn more about Prema at www.Soulutionary.com.

Want to learn even more about your SACRED WEALTH CODE® and continue your work with Prema?

RESOURCES

SACRED WEALTH CODE READINGS

www.SacredWealthCode.com/reading

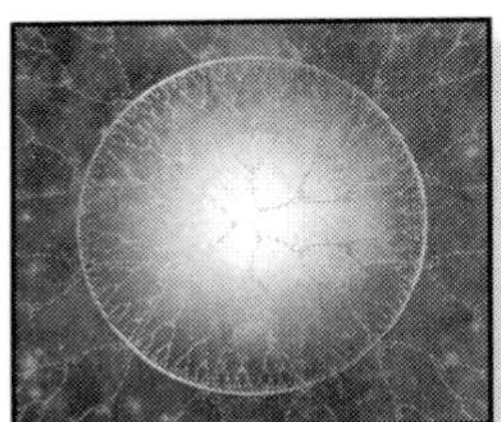

If you want to discover which Archetypes are encoded in your soul blueprint, learn more about your Wealth Council, and align your life and work using Prema's revolutionary Soul Success Map, you need a Sacred Wealth Code Reading!

THE SACRED WEALTH CODE QUIZ

www.SacredWealthCode.com

Take the Sacred Wealth Code Quiz and discover one of your Archetypes!

THE SACRED WEALTH CODE ON FACEBOOK

bit.ly/facebookswc

Join our Facebook group to get live trainings with Prema!

JOIN THE SACRED WEALTH CIRCLE

www.SacredWealthCode.com/circle

Work with Prema in a community of heart-centered seekers to discover, activate, and integrate your Sacred Wealth Code™!

CONTACT PREMA

prema@soulutionary.com • 206.801.0863